Bless
the Lord,
O My Soul

Published by Christian Art Publishers

PO Box 1599, Vereeniging, 1930, RSA

© 2016

First edition 2016

© Three Streams Publishers, Bloomingdale, USA

Cover designed by Christian Art Publishers

Images used under license from Shutterstock.com

Printed in China

ISBN 978-1-4321-1690-3

16   17   18   19   20   21   22   23   24   25   –   10   9   8   7   6   5   4   3   2   1

Bless the Lord, O My Soul

CHRISTIAN ART
PUBLISHERS

Bless the Lord,

O my soul,

and all that is within me,

bless his holy name!

Bless the Lord, O my soul,

and forget not all his benefits,

who forgives all your iniquity,

who heals all your diseases,

who redeems your life from the pit,

who crowns you with

steadfast love and mercy,

who satisfies you with good

so that your youth is renewed like the eagle's.

Psalm 103:1-5

INTRODUCTION

For God is the King of all the earth;
sing praises with a psalm!
~ Psalm 47:7

Throughout the ages believers have found encouragement, consolation, inspiration and guidance from the Psalms. Its wisdom and eternal truths remain steadfast in an ever-changing world. Today we are still able to join with the psalmists in songs of praise and thanksgiving to God. We identify with their heartfelt cries and petitions and our hearts soar in praise to God through their songs of hope and worship.

Bless the Lord, O My Soul provides a resting place amidst the busyness of life today. The short daily readings from Psalms offer you refreshment and tranquility as you spend a few moments reading and meditating on God's Word. The 52 illustrated pages allow you to be creative as you reflect on the designed Scripture verses and color them in if you wish.

Take a few moments and let your soul find peace and renewal in God's Word. Praise Him for his benefits and his steadfast love and mercy. He satisfies you with good things, so sing praises to Him with a psalm!

JANUARY 1

~ Psalm 1

The Way of the *Righteous* and the Wicked

1 Blessed is the man
who walks not in the counsel of the wicked,
nor stands in the way of sinners,
nor sits in the seat of scoffers;
2 but his delight is in the law of the LORD,
and on his law he meditates day and night.

3 He is like a tree
planted by streams of water
that yields its fruit in its season,
and its leaf does not wither.
In all that he does, he prospers.
4 The wicked are not so,
but are like chaff that the wind drives away.

5 Therefore the wicked will not stand in the judgment,
nor sinners in the congregation of the righteous;
6 for the LORD knows the way of the righteous,
but the way of the wicked will perish.

Reflection

JANUARY 2
~ Psalm 2:1-6

The Reign of the Lord's Anointed

1 Why do the nations rage
    and the peoples plot in vain?
2 The kings of the earth set themselves,
    and the rulers take counsel together,
    against the LORD and against his Anointed, saying,
3 "Let us burst their bonds apart
    and cast away their cords from us."

4 He who sits in the heavens laughs;
    the Lord holds them in derision.
5 Then he will speak to them in his wrath,
    and terrify them in his fury, saying,
6 "As for me, I have set my King
    on Zion, my holy hill."

Reflection

JANUARY 3
~ Psalm 2:7-12

7   I will tell of the decree:
    The LORD said to me, "You are my Son;
        today I have begotten you.
8   Ask of me, and I will make the nations your heritage,
        and the ends of the earth your possession.
9   You shall break them with a rod of iron
        and dash them in pieces like a potter's vessel."

10   Now therefore, O kings, be wise;
        be warned, O rulers of the earth.
11   Serve the LORD with fear,
        and rejoice with trembling.
12   Kiss the Son,
        lest he be angry, and you perish in the way,
        for his wrath is quickly kindled.
    Blessed are all who take refuge in him.

Reflection

JANUARY 4
~ Psalm 3

Save Me, O My God

A Psalm of David, when he fled from Absalom his son.

1   O LORD, how many are my foes!
        Many are rising against me;
2   many are saying of my soul,
        "There is no salvation for him in God."   *Selah*

3   But you, O LORD, are a shield about me,
        my glory, and the lifter of my head.
4   I cried aloud to the LORD,
        and he answered me from his holy hill.   *Selah*

5   I lay down and slept;
        I woke again, for the LORD sustained me.
6   I will not be afraid of many thousands of people
        who have set themselves against me all around.

7   Arise, O LORD!
        Save me, O my God!
    For you strike all my enemies on the cheek;
        you break the teeth of the wicked.

8   Salvation belongs to the LORD;
        your blessing be on your people!   *Selah*

Reflection

JANUARY 5
~ Psalm 4

Answer Me When I Call

To the choirmaster: with stringed instruments. A Psalm of David.

1 Answer me when I call, O God of my righteousness!
   You have given me relief when I was in distress.
   Be gracious to me and hear my prayer!

2 O men, how long shall my honor be turned into shame?
   How long will you love vain words and seek
      after lies?   *Selah*

3 But know that the LORD has set apart the godly for himself;
   the LORD hears when I call to him.

4 Be angry, and do not sin;
   ponder in your own hearts on your beds,
      and be silent.   *Selah*

5 Offer right sacrifices,
   and put your trust in the LORD.

6 There are many who say, "Who will show us some good?
   Lift up the light of your face upon us, O LORD!"

7 You have put more joy in my heart
   than they have when their grain and wine abound.

8 In peace I will both lie down and sleep;
   for you alone, O LORD, make me dwell in safety.

Reflection

JANUARY 6
~ Psalm 5:1-6

Lead Me in Your **Righteousness**

To the choirmaster: for the flutes. A Psalm of David.

1 Give ear to my words, O LORD;
  consider my groaning.
2 Give attention to the sound of my cry,
  my King and my God,
  for to you do I pray.
3 O LORD, in the morning you hear my voice;
  in the morning I prepare a sacrifice for you and watch.

4 For you are not a God who delights in wickedness;
  evil may not dwell with you.
5 The boastful shall not stand before your eyes;
  you hate all evildoers.
6 You destroy those who speak lies;
  the LORD abhors the bloodthirsty and deceitful man.

Reflection

_____

_____

_____

_____

_____

_____

_____

JANUARY 7
~ Psalm 5:7-12

7 But I, through the abundance of your steadfast love,
    will enter your house.
I will bow down toward your holy temple
    in the fear of you.
8 Lead me, O LORD, in your righteousness
    because of my enemies;
    make your way straight before me.

9 For there is no truth in their mouth;
    their inmost self is destruction;
their throat is an open grave;
    they flatter with their tongue.
10 Make them bear their guilt, O God;
    let them fall by their own counsels;
because of the abundance of their transgressions
        cast them out,
    for they have rebelled against you.

11 But let all who take refuge in you rejoice;
    let them ever sing for joy,
and spread your protection over them,
    that those who love your name may exult in you.
12 For you bless the righteous, O LORD;
    you cover him with favor as with a shield.

Reflection

In
peace
I will both
lie down
& sleep;
for you alone,
O Lord,
make me dwell
in safety.
Psalm 4:8

JANUARY 8
~ Psalm 6:1-5

O Lord, Deliver My Life

To the choirmaster: with stringed instruments; according to The Sheminith.
A Psalm of David.

1   O Lord, rebuke me not in your anger,
        nor discipline me in your wrath.
2   Be gracious to me, O Lord, for I am languishing;
        heal me, O Lord, for my bones are troubled.
3   My soul also is greatly troubled.
        But you, O Lord—how long?

4   Turn, O Lord, deliver my life;
        save me for the sake of your steadfast love.
5   For in death there is no remembrance of you;
        in Sheol who will give you praise?

Reflection

JANUARY 9
~ Psalm 6:6-10

6   I am weary with my moaning;
       every night I flood my bed with tears;
       I drench my couch with my weeping.

7   My eye wastes away because of grief;
       it grows weak because of all my foes.

8   Depart from me, all you workers of evil,
       for the LORD has heard the sound of my weeping.

9   The LORD has heard my plea;
       the LORD accepts my prayer.

10   All my enemies shall be ashamed and greatly troubled;
       they shall turn back and be put to shame in a moment.

Reflection

JANUARY 10
~ Psalm 7:1-7

In You Do I *Take Refuge*

A Shiggaion of David, which he sang to the LORD concerning the words of Cush, a Benjaminite.

1 O LORD my God, in you do I take refuge;
   save me from all my pursuers and deliver me,
2 lest like a lion they tear my soul apart,
   rending it in pieces, with none to deliver.

3 O LORD my God, if I have done this,
   if there is wrong in my hands,
4 if I have repaid my friend with evil
   or plundered my enemy without cause,
5 let the enemy pursue my soul and overtake it,
   and let him trample my life to the ground
   and lay my glory in the dust.   *Selah*

6 Arise, O LORD, in your anger;
   lift yourself up against the fury of my enemies;
   awake for me; you have appointed a judgment.
7 Let the assembly of the peoples be gathered about you;
   over it return on high.

Reflection

JANUARY 11
~ Psalm 7:8-11

8   The LORD judges the peoples;
        judge me, O LORD, according to my righteousness
        and according to the integrity that is in me.

9   Oh, let the evil of the wicked come to an end,
        and may you establish the righteous—
    you who test the minds and hearts,
        O righteous God!

10   My shield is with God,
        who saves the upright in heart.

11   God is a righteous judge,
        and a God who feels indignation every day.

Reflection

JANUARY 12
~ Psalm 7:12-17

12   If a man does not repent, God will whet his sword;
       he has bent and readied his bow;
13   he has prepared for him his deadly weapons,
       making his arrows fiery shafts.
14   Behold, the wicked man conceives evil
       and is pregnant with mischief
       and gives birth to lies.
15   He makes a pit, digging it out,
       and falls into the hole that he has made.
16   His mischief returns upon his own head,
       and on his own skull his violence descends.

17   I will give to the LORD the thanks due to his righteousness,
       and I will sing praise to the name of the LORD,
       the Most High.

Reflection

JANUARY 13
~ Psalm 8

How Majestic Is Your Name

To the choirmaster: according to The Gittith. A Psalm of David.

1 O LORD, our Lord,
    how majestic is your name in all the earth!
You have set your glory above the heavens.
2   Out of the mouth of babies and infants,
you have established strength because of your foes,
    to still the enemy and the avenger.

3 When I look at your heavens, the work of your fingers,
    the moon and the stars, which you have set in place,
4 what is man that you are mindful of him,
    and the son of man that you care for him?

5 Yet you have made him a little lower than the heavenly beings
    and crowned him with glory and honor.
6 You have given him dominion over the works of your hands;
    you have put all things under his feet,
7 all sheep and oxen,
    and also the beasts of the field,
8 the birds of the heavens, and the fish of the sea,
    whatever passes along the paths of the seas.

9 O LORD, our Lord,
    how majestic is your name in all the earth!

Reflection

JANUARY 14
~ Psalm 9:1-6

I Will Recount *Your Wonderful Deeds*

To the choirmaster: according to Muth-labben. A Psalm of David.

1 I will give thanks to the LORD with my whole heart;
   I will recount all of your wonderful deeds.
2 I will be glad and exult in you;
   I will sing praise to your name, O Most High.

3 When my enemies turn back,
   they stumble and perish before your presence.
4 For you have maintained my just cause;
   you have sat on the throne, giving righteous judgment.

5 You have rebuked the nations; you have made
   the wicked perish;
   you have blotted out their name forever and ever.
6 The enemy came to an end in everlasting ruins;
   their cities you rooted out;
   the very memory of them has perished.

Reflection

When I look at your

heavens,

the work of your fingers,

the moon &

the stars,

which you have set
in place, what is *man*

that you are

mindful of him, and

the son of man

that you *care*

for him?

Ps. 8:3-4

JANUARY 15
~ Psalm 9:7-12

7   But the LORD sits enthroned forever;
     he has established his throne for justice,
8   and he judges the world with righteousness;
     he judges the peoples with uprightness.

9   The LORD is a stronghold for the oppressed,
     a stronghold in times of trouble.
10   And those who know your name put their trust in you,
     for you, O LORD, have not forsaken those who seek you.

11   Sing praises to the LORD, who sits enthroned in Zion!
     Tell among the peoples his deeds!
12   For he who avenges blood is mindful of them;
     he does not forget the cry of the afflicted.

Reflection

JANUARY 16
~ Psalm 9:13-20

13   Be gracious to me, O LORD!
        See my affliction from those who hate me,
        O you who lift me up from the gates of death,
14   that I may recount all your praises,
        that in the gates of the daughter of Zion
        I may rejoice in your salvation.

15   The nations have sunk in the pit that they made;
        in the net that they hid, their own foot has been caught.
16   The LORD has made himself known; he has
        executed judgment;
        the wicked are snared in the work of their own hands.

Higgaion. Selah

17   The wicked shall return to Sheol,
        all the nations that forget God.

18   For the needy shall not always be forgotten,
        and the hope of the poor shall not perish forever.

19   Arise, O LORD! Let not man prevail;
        let the nations be judged before you!
20   Put them in fear, O LORD!
        Let the nations know that they are but men!   *Selah*

Reflection

JANUARY 17
~ Psalm 10:1-6

Why Do You Hide *Yourself*?

1 Why, O LORD, do you stand far away?
   Why do you hide yourself in times of trouble?

2 In arrogance the wicked hotly pursue the poor;
   let them be caught in the schemes that they have devised.

3 For the wicked boasts of the desires of his soul,
   and the one greedy for gain curses and renounces
      the LORD.

4 In the pride of his face the wicked does not seek him;
   all his thoughts are, "There is no God."

5 His ways prosper at all times;
   your judgments are on high, out of his sight;
   as for all his foes, he puffs at them.

6 He says in his heart, "I shall not be moved;
   throughout all generations I shall not meet adversity."

Reflection

JANUARY 18
~ Psalm 10:7-11

7   His mouth is filled with cursing and deceit and oppression;
        under his tongue are mischief and iniquity.

8   He sits in ambush in the villages;
        in hiding places he murders the innocent.
    His eyes stealthily watch for the helpless;

9   he lurks in ambush like a lion in his thicket;
    he lurks that he may seize the poor;
        he seizes the poor when he draws him into his net.

10   The helpless are crushed, sink down,
        and fall by his might.

11   He says in his heart, "God has forgotten,
        he has hidden his face, he will never see it."

Reflection

JANUARY 19
~ Psalm 10:12-18

12   Arise, O Lord; O God, lift up your hand;
        forget not the afflicted.
13   Why does the wicked renounce God
        and say in his heart, "You will not call to account"?
14   But you do see, for you note mischief and vexation,
        that you may take it into your hands;
     to you the helpless commits himself;
        you have been the helper of the fatherless.
15   Break the arm of the wicked and evildoer;
        call his wickedness to account till you find none.

16   The Lord is king forever and ever;
        the nations perish from his land.
17   O Lord, you hear the desire of the afflicted;
        you will strengthen their heart; you will incline your ear
18   to do justice to the fatherless and the oppressed,
        so that man who is of the earth may strike terror no more.

Reflection

JANUARY 20
~ Psalm 11

The Lord Is in His Holy Temple

To the choirmaster. Of David.

1   In the LORD I take refuge;
how can you say to my soul,
    " Flee like a bird to your mountain,
2   for behold, the wicked bend the bow;
    they have fitted their arrow to the string
    to shoot in the dark at the upright in heart;
3   if the foundations are destroyed,
    what can the righteous do?"

4   The LORD is in his holy temple;
    the LORD's throne is in heaven;
    his eyes see, his eyelids test the children of man.
5   The LORD tests the righteous,
    but his soul hates the wicked and the one who
     loves violence.
6   Let him rain coals on the wicked;
    fire and sulfur and a scorching wind shall be
     the portion of their cup.
7   For the LORD is righteous;
he loves righteous deeds;
    the upright shall behold his face.

Reflection

JANUARY 21
~ Psalm 12

The Faithful Have Vanished

To the choirmaster: according to The Sheminith. A Psalm of David.

1 Save, O Lord, for the godly one is gone;
  for the faithful have vanished from among the
      children of man.
2 Everyone utters lies to his neighbor;
  with flattering lips and a double heart they speak.

3 May the Lord cut off all flattering lips,
  the tongue that makes great boasts,
4 those who say, "With our tongue we will prevail,
  our lips are with us; who is master over us?"

5 " Because the poor are plundered, because the needy groan,
  I will now arise," says the Lord;
  " I will place him in the safety for which he longs."
6 The words of the Lord are pure words,
  like silver refined in a furnace on the ground,
      purified seven times.

7 You, O Lord, will keep them;
  you will guard us from this generation forever.
8 On every side the wicked prowl,
  as vileness is exalted among the children of man.

Reflection

I will give *thanks* to the *LORD* with my *whole heart;* I will recount all of your *wonderful deeds.* I will be glad and exult in you; I will sing *praise* to your name, *O Most High.*

Psalm 9:1-2

JANUARY 22
~ Psalm 13

How Long, O Lord?

To the choirmaster. A Psalm of David.

1 How long, O LORD? Will you forget me forever?
   How long will you hide your face from me?
2 How long must I take counsel in my soul
   and have sorrow in my heart all the day?
   How long shall my enemy be exalted over me?

3 Consider and answer me, O LORD my God;
   light up my eyes, lest I sleep the sleep of death,
4 lest my enemy say, "I have prevailed over him,"
   lest my foes rejoice because I am shaken.

5 But I have trusted in your steadfast love;
   my heart shall rejoice in your salvation.
6 I will sing to the LORD,
   because he has dealt bountifully with me.

Reflection

JANUARY 23
~ Psalm 14
The Fool Says, There Is No God

To the choirmaster. Of David.

1 The fool says in his heart, "There is no God."
　　They are corrupt, they do abominable deeds;
　　there is none who does good.

2 The LORD looks down from heaven on the children of man,
　　to see if there are any who understand,
　　who seek after God.

3 They have all turned aside; together they have
　　　　become corrupt;
　　there is none who does good,
　　not even one.

4 Have they no knowledge, all the evildoers
　　who eat up my people as they eat bread
　　and do not call upon the LORD?

5 There they are in great terror,
　　for God is with the generation of the righteous.
6 You would shame the plans of the poor,
　　but the LORD is his refuge.

7 Oh, that salvation for Israel would come out of Zion!
　　When the LORD restores the fortunes of his people,
　　let Jacob rejoice, let Israel be glad.

Reflection

_____

_____

_____

_____

JANUARY 24
~ Psalm 15

Who Shall Dwell on Your *Holy Hill?*

A Psalm of David.

1   O Lord, who shall sojourn in your tent?
       Who shall dwell on your holy hill?

2   He who walks blamelessly and does what is right
       and speaks truth in his heart;
3   who does not slander with his tongue
       and does no evil to his neighbor,
         nor takes up a reproach against his friend;
4   in whose eyes a vile person is despised,
       but who honors those who fear the Lord;
     who swears to his own hurt and does not change;
5   who does not put out his money at interest
         and does not take a bribe against the innocent.
     He who does these things shall never be moved.

Reflection

JANUARY 25
~ Psalm 16:1-6

You Will Not Abandon My Soul

A Miktam of David.

1 Preserve me, O God, for in you I take refuge.
2 I say to the LORD, "You are my Lord;
    I have no good apart from you."

3 As for the saints in the land, they are the excellent ones,
    in whom is all my delight.

4 The sorrows of those who run after another god
        shall multiply;
    their drink offerings of blood I will not pour out
    or take their names on my lips.

5 The LORD is my chosen portion and my cup;
    you hold my lot.
6 The lines have fallen for me in pleasant places;
    indeed, I have a beautiful inheritance.

Reflection

JANUARY 26
~ Psalm 16:7-11

7   I bless the LORD who gives me counsel;
      in the night also my heart instructs me.

8   I have set the LORD always before me;
      because he is at my right hand, I shall not be shaken.

9   Therefore my heart is glad, and my whole being rejoices;
      my flesh also dwells secure.

10   For you will not abandon my soul to Sheol,
      or let your holy one see corruption.

11   You make known to me the path of life;
      in your presence there is fullness of joy;
      at your right hand are pleasures forevermore.

Reflection

JANUARY 27
~ Psalm 17:1-5

In the *Shadow of Your Wings*

A Prayer of David.

1   Hear a just cause, O LORD; attend to my cry!
    Give ear to my prayer from lips free of deceit!
2   From your presence let my vindication come!
    Let your eyes behold the right!

3   You have tried my heart, you have visited me by night,
    you have tested me, and you will find nothing;
    I have purposed that my mouth will not transgress.
4   With regard to the works of man, by the word of your lips
    I have avoided the ways of the violent.
5   My steps have held fast to your paths;
    my feet have not slipped.

Reflection

JANUARY 28
~ Psalm 17:6-9

6   I call upon you, for you will answer me, O God;
       incline your ear to me; hear my words.
7   Wondrously show your steadfast love,
       O Savior of those who seek refuge
       from their adversaries at your right hand.

8   Keep me as the apple of your eye;
       hide me in the shadow of your wings,
9   from the wicked who do me violence,
       my deadly enemies who surround me.

Reflection

You make *known to me* the path *of life;* in your *presence* there is *fullness* of *joy;* at your right hand are *pleasures forevermore.*

Psalm 16:11

JANUARY 29
~ Psalm 17:10-15

10   They close their hearts to pity;
         with their mouths they speak arrogantly.
11   They have now surrounded our steps;
         they set their eyes to cast us to the ground.
12   He is like a lion eager to tear,
         as a young lion lurking in ambush.

13   Arise, O LORD! Confront him, subdue him!
         Deliver my soul from the wicked by your sword,
14   from men by your hand, O LORD,
         from men of the world whose portion is in this life.
     You fill their womb with treasure;
         they are satisfied with children,
         and they leave their abundance to their infants.

15   As for me, I shall behold your face in righteousness;
         when I awake, I shall be satisfied with your likeness.

Reflection

JANUARY 30
~ Psalm 18:1-8

The LORD is My Rock and My Fortress

To the choirmaster. A Psalm of David, the servant of the LORD, who addressed the words of this song to the LORD on the day when the LORD delivered him from the hand of all his enemies, and from the hand of Saul. He said:

1   I love you, O LORD, my strength.
2   The LORD is my rock and my fortress and my deliverer,
    my God, my rock, in whom I take refuge,
    my shield, and the horn of my salvation, my stronghold.
3   I call upon the LORD, who is worthy to be praised,
    and I am saved from my enemies.

4   The cords of death encompassed me;
    the torrents of destruction assailed me;
5   the cords of Sheol entangled me;
    the snares of death confronted me.

6   In my distress I called upon the LORD;
    to my God I cried for help.
    From his temple he heard my voice,
    and my cry to him reached his ears.

7   Then the earth reeled and rocked;
    the foundations also of the mountains trembled
    and quaked, because he was angry.
8   Smoke went up from his nostrils,
    and devouring fire from his mouth;
    glowing coals flamed forth from him.

Reflection

JANUARY 31
~ Psalm 18:9-17

9 He bowed the heavens and came down;
  thick darkness was under his feet.
10 He rode on a cherub and flew;
  he came swiftly on the wings of the wind.
11 He made darkness his covering, his canopy around him,
  thick clouds dark with water.
12 Out of the brightness before him
  hailstones and coals of fire broke through his clouds.

13 The LORD also thundered in the heavens,
  and the Most High uttered his voice,
  hailstones and coals of fire.
14 And he sent out his arrows and scattered them;
  he flashed forth lightnings and routed them.
15 Then the channels of the sea were seen,
  and the foundations of the world were laid bare
 at your rebuke, O LORD,
  at the blast of the breath of your nostrils.

16 He sent from on high, he took me;
  he drew me out of many waters.
17 He rescued me from my strong enemy
  and from those who hated me,
  for they were too mighty for me.

Reflection

FEBRUARY 1
~ Psalm 18:18-24

18   They confronted me in the day of my calamity,
        but the LORD was my support.
19   He brought me out into a broad place;
        he rescued me, because he delighted in me.

20   The LORD dealt with me according to my righteousness;
        according to the cleanness of my hands he rewarded me.
21   For I have kept the ways of the LORD,
        and have not wickedly departed from my God.
22   For all his rules were before me,
        and his statutes I did not put away from me.
23   I was blameless before him,
        and I kept myself from my guilt.
24   So the LORD has rewarded me according to my righteousness,
        according to the cleanness of my hands in his sight.

Reflection

FEBRUARY 2
~ Psalm 18:25-32

25   With the merciful you show yourself merciful;
        with the blameless man you show yourself blameless;
26   with the purified you show yourself pure;
        and with the crooked you make yourself seem tortuous.
27   For you save a humble people,
        but the haughty eyes you bring down.
28   For it is you who light my lamp;
        the LORD my God lightens my darkness.
29   For by you I can run against a troop,
        and by my God I can leap over a wall.
30   This God—his way is perfect;
        the word of the LORD proves true;
        he is a shield for all those who take refuge in him.

31   For who is God, but the LORD?
        And who is a rock, except our God?—
32   the God who equipped me with strength
        and made my way blameless.

Reflection

FEBRUARY 3
~ Psalm 18:33-39

33   He made my feet like the feet of a deer
      and set me secure on the heights.
34   He trains my hands for war,
      so that my arms can bend a bow of bronze.
35   You have given me the shield of your salvation,
      and your right hand supported me,
      and your gentleness made me great.
36   You gave a wide place for my steps under me,
      and my feet did not slip.
37   I pursued my enemies and overtook them,
      and did not turn back till they were consumed.
38   I thrust them through, so that they were not able to rise;
      they fell under my feet.
39   For you equipped me with strength for the battle;
      you made those who rise against me sink under me.

Reflection

FEBRUARY 4
~ Psalm 18:40-45

40   You made my enemies turn their backs to me,
        and those who hated me I destroyed.
41   They cried for help, but there was none to save;
        they cried to the LORD, but he did not answer them.
42   I beat them fine as dust before the wind;
        I cast them out like the mire of the streets.

43   You delivered me from strife with the people;
        you made me the head of the nations;
        people whom I had not known served me.
44   As soon as they heard of me they obeyed me;
        foreigners came cringing to me.
45   Foreigners lost heart
        and came trembling out of their fortresses.

Reflection

I love you, O LORD, my strength. The LORD is my rock and my fortress and my deliverer, my God, my rock, in whom I take refuge, my shield, and the horn of my salvation, my stronghold.

Psalm 18:1-2

FEBRUARY 5
~ Psalm 18:46-50

46   The LORD lives, and blessed be my rock,
         and exalted be the God of my salvation—
47   the God who gave me vengeance
         and subdued peoples under me,
48   who rescued me from my enemies;
         yes, you exalted me above those who rose against me;
         you delivered me from the man of violence.

49   For this I will praise you, O LORD, among the nations,
         and sing to your name.
50   Great salvation he brings to his king,
         and shows steadfast love to his anointed,
         to David and his offspring forever.

Reflection

FEBRUARY 6
~ Psalm 19:1-6

The Law of the Lord Is Perfect

To the choirmaster. A Psalm of David.

1 The heavens declare the glory of God,
  and the sky above proclaims his handiwork.
2 Day to day pours out speech,
  and night to night reveals knowledge.
3 There is no speech, nor are there words,
  whose voice is not heard.
4 Their voice goes out through all the earth,
  and their words to the end of the world.
  In them he has set a tent for the sun,
5   which comes out like a bridegroom leaving his chamber,
  and, like a strong man, runs its course with joy.
6 Its rising is from the end of the heavens,
  and its circuit to the end of them,
  and there is nothing hidden from its heat.

Reflection

FEBRUARY 7
~ Psalm 19:7-14

7   The law of the LORD is perfect,
      reviving the soul;
    the testimony of the LORD is sure,
      making wise the simple;

8   the precepts of the LORD are right,
      rejoicing the heart;
    the commandment of the LORD is pure,
      enlightening the eyes;

9   the fear of the LORD is clean,
      enduring forever;
    the rules of the LORD are true,
      and righteous altogether.

10   More to be desired are they than gold,
      even much fine gold;
    sweeter also than honey
      and drippings of the honeycomb.

11   Moreover, by them is your servant warned;
      in keeping them there is great reward.

12   Who can discern his errors?
      Declare me innocent from hidden faults.

13   Keep back your servant also from presumptuous sins;
      let them not have dominion over me!
    Then I shall be blameless,
      and innocent of great transgression.

14   Let the words of my mouth and the meditation of my heart
      be acceptable in your sight,
      O LORD, my rock and my redeemer.

Reflection

FEBRUARY 8
~ Psalm 20

Trust in the Name of the Lord Our God

To the choirmaster. A Psalm of David.

1 May the LORD answer you in the day of trouble!
   May the name of the God of Jacob protect you!
2 May he send you help from the sanctuary
   and give you support from Zion!
3 May he remember all your offerings
   and regard with favor your burnt sacrifices!   *Selah*

4 May he grant you your heart's desire
   and fulfill all your plans!
5 May we shout for joy over your salvation,
   and in the name of our God set up our banners!
   May the LORD fulfill all your petitions!

6 Now I know that the LORD saves his anointed;
   he will answer him from his holy heaven
   with the saving might of his right hand.
7 Some trust in chariots and some in horses,
   but we trust in the name of the LORD our God.
8 They collapse and fall,
   but we rise and stand upright.

9 O LORD, save the king!
   May he answer us when we call.

Reflection

FEBRUARY 9
~ Psalm 21:1-7

The King Rejoices in the Lord's Strength

To the choirmaster. A Psalm of David.

1   O Lord, in your strength the king rejoices,
     and in your salvation how greatly he exults!

2   You have given him his heart's desire
     and have not withheld the request of his lips.   *Selah*

3   For you meet him with rich blessings;
     you set a crown of fine gold upon his head.

4   He asked life of you; you gave it to him,
     length of days forever and ever.

5   His glory is great through your salvation;
     splendor and majesty you bestow on him.

6   For you make him most blessed forever;
     you make him glad with the joy of your presence.

7   For the king trusts in the Lord,
     and through the steadfast love of the Most High
     he shall not be moved.

Reflection

FEBRUARY 10
~ Psalm 21:8-13

8   Your hand will find out all your enemies;
        your right hand will find out those who hate you.

9   You will make them as a blazing oven
        when you appear.
The LORD will swallow them up in his wrath,
        and fire will consume them.

10   You will destroy their descendants from the earth,
        and their offspring from among the children of man.

11   Though they plan evil against you,
        though they devise mischief, they will not succeed.

12   For you will put them to flight;
        you will aim at their faces with your bows.

13   Be exalted, O LORD, in your strength!
        We will sing and praise your power.

Reflection

FEBRUARY 11
~ Psalm 22:1-5

Why Have You Forsaken *Me?*

To the choirmaster: according to The Doe of the Dawn. A Psalm of David.

1 My God, my God, why have you forsaken me?
    Why are you so far from saving me, from the words of
        my groaning?
2 O my God, I cry by day, but you do not answer,
    and by night, but I find no rest.

3 Yet you are holy,
    enthroned on the praises of Israel.
4 In you our fathers trusted;
    they trusted, and you delivered them.
5 To you they cried and were rescued;
    in you they trusted and were not put to shame.

Reflection

Let the words of my mouth and the meditation of *my* **heart** be acceptable in *your sight,* ***O Lord,*** *my rock* and my ***redeemer.***

Psalm 19:14

FEBRUARY 12
~ Psalm 22:6-11

6   But I am a worm and not a man,
        scorned by mankind and despised by the people.
7   All who see me mock me;
        they make mouths at me; they wag their heads;
8   " He trusts in the LORD; let him deliver him;
        let him rescue him, for he delights in him!"

9   Yet you are he who took me from the womb;
        you made me trust you at my mother's breasts.
10   On you was I cast from my birth,
        and from my mother's womb you have been my God.
11   Be not far from me,
        for trouble is near,
        and there is none to help.

Reflection

FEBRUARY 13
~ Psalm 22:12-18

12 Many bulls encompass me;
   strong bulls of Bashan surround me;
13 they open wide their mouths at me,
   like a ravening and roaring lion.

14 I am poured out like water,
   and all my bones are out of joint;
 my heart is like wax;
   it is melted within my breast;
15 my strength is dried up like a potsherd,
   and my tongue sticks to my jaws;
   you lay me in the dust of death.

16 For dogs encompass me;
   a company of evildoers encircles me;
 they have pierced my hands and feet—
17 I can count all my bones—
 they stare and gloat over me;
18 they divide my garments among them,
   and for my clothing they cast lots.

Reflection

FEBRUARY 14
~ Psalm 22:19-24

19   But you, O LORD, do not be far off!
        O you my help, come quickly to my aid!
20   Deliver my soul from the sword,
        my precious life from the power of the dog!
21   Save me from the mouth of the lion!
    You have rescued me from the horns of the wild oxen!

22   I will tell of your name to my brothers;
        in the midst of the congregation I will praise you:
23   You who fear the LORD, praise him!
        All you offspring of Jacob, glorify him,
        and stand in awe of him, all you offspring of Israel!
24   For he has not despised or abhorred
        the affliction of the afflicted,
    and he has not hidden his face from him,
        but has heard, when he cried to him.

Reflection

FEBRUARY 15
~ Psalm 22:25-31

25   From you comes my praise in the great congregation;
        my vows I will perform before those who fear him.
26   The afflicted shall eat and be satisfied;
        those who seek him shall praise the LORD!
        May your hearts live forever!

27   All the ends of the earth shall remember
        and turn to the LORD,
    and all the families of the nations
        shall worship before you.
28   For kingship belongs to the LORD,
        and he rules over the nations.

29   All the prosperous of the earth eat and worship;
        before him shall bow all who go down to the dust,
        even the one who could not keep himself alive.
30   Posterity shall serve him;
        it shall be told of the Lord to the coming generation;
31   they shall come and proclaim his righteousness to a people
        yet unborn,
        that he has done it.

Reflection

FEBRUARY 16
~ Psalm 23

The Lord Is My *Shepherd*

A Psalm of David.

1 The LORD is my shepherd; I shall not want.
2   He makes me lie down in green pastures.
He leads me beside still waters.
3   He restores my soul.
He leads me in paths of righteousness
    for his name's sake.

4   Even though I walk through the valley of the
        shadow of death,
    I will fear no evil,
for you are with me;
    your rod and your staff,
    they comfort me.

5   You prepare a table before me
    in the presence of my enemies;
you anoint my head with oil;
    my cup overflows.
6   Surely goodness and mercy shall follow me
    all the days of my life,
and I shall dwell in the house of the LORD
    forever.

Reflection

FEBRUARY 17
~ Psalm 24:1-6

The King of Glory

A Psalm of David.

1 The earth is the LORD's and the fullness thereof,
   the world and those who dwell therein,
2 for he has founded it upon the seas
   and established it upon the rivers.

3 Who shall ascend the hill of the LORD?
   And who shall stand in his holy place?
4 He who has clean hands and a pure heart,
   who does not lift up his soul to what is false
   and does not swear deceitfully.
5 He will receive blessing from the LORD
   and righteousness from the God of his salvation.
6 Such is the generation of those who seek him,
   who seek the face of the God of Jacob.   *Selah*

Reflection

FEBRUARY 18
~ Psalm 24:7-10

7   Lift up your heads, O gates!
        And be lifted up, O ancient doors,
        that the King of glory may come in.

8   Who is this King of glory?
        The LORD, strong and mighty,
        the LORD, mighty in battle!

9   Lift up your heads, O gates!
        And lift them up, O ancient doors,
        that the King of glory may come in.

10   Who is this King of glory?
        The LORD of hosts,
        he is the King of glory!   *Selah*

Reflection

The LORD is my shepherd; I shall not want. He makes me lie down in green pastures. He leads me beside still waters. He restores my soul.

Psalm 23:1-3

FEBRUARY 19
~ Psalm 25:1-5

Teach Me Your Paths

Of David.

1 To you, O LORD, I lift up my soul.
2 O my God, in you I trust;
        let me not be put to shame;
        let not my enemies exult over me.
3 Indeed, none who wait for you shall be put to shame;
        they shall be ashamed who are wantonly treacherous.

4 Make me to know your ways, O LORD;
        teach me your paths.
5 Lead me in your truth and teach me,
        for you are the God of my salvation;
        for you I wait all the day long.

Reflection

FEBRUARY 20
~ Psalm 25:6-10

6   Remember your mercy, O LORD, and your steadfast love,
         for they have been from of old.

7   Remember not the sins of my youth or my transgressions;
         according to your steadfast love remember me,
         for the sake of your goodness, O LORD!

8   Good and upright is the LORD;
         therefore he instructs sinners in the way.

9   He leads the humble in what is right,
         and teaches the humble his way.

10   All the paths of the LORD are steadfast love and faithfulness,
         for those who keep his covenant and his testimonies.

Reflection

FEBRUARY 21
~ Psalm 25:11-15

11   For your name's sake, O Lord,
        pardon my guilt, for it is great.

12   Who is the man who fears the Lord?
        Him will he instruct in the way that he should choose.

13   His soul shall abide in well-being,
        and his offspring shall inherit the land.

14   The friendship of the Lord is for those who fear him,
        and he makes known to them his covenant.

15   My eyes are ever toward the Lord,
        for he will pluck my feet out of the net.

Reflection

FEBRUARY 22
~ Psalm 25:16-22

16   Turn to me and be gracious to me,
        for I am lonely and afflicted.
17   The troubles of my heart are enlarged;
        bring me out of my distresses.
18   Consider my affliction and my trouble,
        and forgive all my sins.

19   Consider how many are my foes,
        and with what violent hatred they hate me.
20   Oh, guard my soul, and deliver me!
        Let me not be put to shame, for I take refuge in you.
21   May integrity and uprightness preserve me,
        for I wait for you.

22   Redeem Israel, O God,
        out of all his troubles.

Reflection

FEBRUARY 23
~ Psalm 26:1-7

I Will *Bless the Lord*

Of David.

1   Vindicate me, O LORD,
     for I have walked in my integrity,
     and I have trusted in the LORD without wavering.
2   Prove me, O LORD, and try me;
     test my heart and my mind.
3   For your steadfast love is before my eyes,
     and I walk in your faithfulness.

4   I do not sit with men of falsehood,
     nor do I consort with hypocrites.
5   I hate the assembly of evildoers,
     and I will not sit with the wicked.

6   I wash my hands in innocence
     and go around your altar, O LORD,
7   proclaiming thanksgiving aloud,
     and telling all your wondrous deeds.

Reflection

FEBRUARY 24
~ Psalm 26:8-12

8   O LORD, I love the habitation of your house
    and the place where your glory dwells.
9   Do not sweep my soul away with sinners,
    nor my life with bloodthirsty men,
10 in whose hands are evil devices,
    and whose right hands are full of bribes.

11 But as for me, I shall walk in my integrity;
    redeem me, and be gracious to me.
12 My foot stands on level ground;
    in the great assembly I will bless the LORD.

Reflection

FEBRUARY 25
~ Psalm 27:1-6

The Lord Is My Light and My Salvation

Of David.

1   The Lord is my light and my salvation;
        whom shall I fear?
    The Lord is the stronghold of my life;
        of whom shall I be afraid?

2   When evildoers assail me
        to eat up my flesh,
    my adversaries and foes,
        it is they who stumble and fall.

3   Though an army encamp against me,
        my heart shall not fear;
    though war arise against me,
        yet I will be confident.

4   One thing have I asked of the Lord,
        that will I seek after:
    that I may dwell in the house of the Lord
        all the days of my life,
    to gaze upon the beauty of the Lord
        and to inquire in his temple.

5   For he will hide me in his shelter
        in the day of trouble;
     he will conceal me under the cover of his tent;
        he will lift me high upon a rock.

6   And now my head shall be lifted up
        above my enemies all around me,
     and I will offer in his tent
        sacrifices with shouts of joy;
     I will sing and make melody to the Lord.

Reflection

_____
_____
_____
_____
_____
_____
_____
_____
_____
_____
_____

Make me to know
your ways,
O Lord;
teach me your paths.
Lead me in your
truth
and teach me, for you are
the God of my
salvation;
for you I wait
all the day long.
Psalm 25:4-5

FEBRUARY 26
~ Psalm 27:7-14

7   Hear, O LORD, when I cry aloud;
      be gracious to me and answer me!
8   You have said, "Seek my face."
    My heart says to you,
      "Your face, LORD, do I seek."
9   Hide not your face from me.
    Turn not your servant away in anger,
      O you who have been my help.
    Cast me not off; forsake me not,
      O God of my salvation!
10   For my father and my mother have forsaken me,
      but the LORD will take me in.

11   Teach me your way, O LORD,
      and lead me on a level path
      because of my enemies.
12   Give me not up to the will of my adversaries;
      for false witnesses have risen against me,
      and they breathe out violence.

13   I believe that I shall look upon the goodness of the LORD
      in the land of the living!
14   Wait for the LORD;
      be strong, and let your heart take courage;
      wait for the LORD!

Reflection

FEBRUARY 27
~ Psalm 28

The Lord Is My Strength and My Shield

Of David.

1   To you, O LORD, I call;
      my rock, be not deaf to me,
    lest, if you be silent to me,
      I become like those who go down to the pit.

2   Hear the voice of my pleas for mercy,
      when I cry to you for help,
    when I lift up my hands
      toward your most holy sanctuary.

3   Do not drag me off with the wicked,
      with the workers of evil,
    who speak peace with their neighbors
      while evil is in their hearts.

4   Give to them according to their work
      and according to the evil of their deeds;
    give to them according to the work of their hands;
      render them their due reward.

5   Because they do not regard the works of the LORD
      or the work of his hands,
    he will tear them down and build them up no more.

6   Blessed be the LORD!
         For he has heard the voice of my pleas for mercy.
7   The LORD is my strength and my shield;
         in him my heart trusts, and I am helped;
     my heart exults,
         and with my song I give thanks to him.

8   The LORD is the strength of his people;
         he is the saving refuge of his anointed.
9   Oh, save your people and bless your heritage!
         Be their shepherd and carry them forever.

Reflection

FEBRUARY 28
~ Psalm 29:1-6

Ascribe to the *Lord Glory*

A Psalm of David.

1   Ascribe to the LORD, O heavenly beings,
      ascribe to the LORD glory and strength.
2   Ascribe to the LORD the glory due his name;
      worship the LORD in the splendor of holiness.

3   The voice of the LORD is over the waters;
      the God of glory thunders,
      the LORD, over many waters.
4   The voice of the LORD is powerful;
      the voice of the LORD is full of majesty.

5   The voice of the LORD breaks the cedars;
      the LORD breaks the cedars of Lebanon.
6   He makes Lebanon to skip like a calf,
      and Sirion like a young wild ox.

Reflection

MARCH 1
~ Psalm 29:7-11

7   The voice of the LORD flashes forth flames of fire.

8   The voice of the LORD shakes the wilderness;
        the LORD shakes the wilderness of Kadesh.

9   The voice of the LORD makes the deer give birth
        and strips the forests bare,
        and in his temple all cry, "Glory!"

10   The LORD sits enthroned over the flood;
        the LORD sits enthroned as king forever.

11   May the LORD give strength to his people!
        May the LORD bless his people with peace!

Reflection

MARCH 2
~ Psalm 30:1-5

Joy Comes with *the Morning*

A Psalm of David. A song at the dedication of the temple.

1   I will extol you, O LORD, for you have drawn me up
     and have not let my foes rejoice over me.
2   O LORD my God, I cried to you for help,
     and you have healed me.
3   O LORD, you have brought up my soul from Sheol;
     you restored me to life from among those who go
     down to the pit.

4   Sing praises to the LORD, O you his saints,
     and give thanks to his holy name.
5   For his anger is but for a moment,
     and his favor is for a lifetime.
     Weeping may tarry for the night,
     but joy comes with the morning.

Reflection

MARCH 3
~ Psalm 30:6-12

6   As for me, I said in my prosperity,
        "I shall never be moved."
7   By your favor, O Lord,
        you made my mountain stand strong;
    you hid your face;
        I was dismayed.

8   To you, O Lord, I cry,
        and to the Lord I plead for mercy:
9   "What profit is there in my death,
        if I go down to the pit?
    Will the dust praise you?
        Will it tell of your faithfulness?
10   Hear, O Lord, and be merciful to me!
        O Lord, be my helper!"

11   You have turned for me my mourning into dancing;
        you have loosed my sackcloth
        and clothed me with gladness,
12   that my glory may sing your praise and not be silent.
        O Lord my God, I will give thanks to you forever!

Reflection

MARCH 4
~ Psalm 31:1-8

Into Your Hand *I Commit My Spirit*

To the choirmaster. A Psalm of David.

1 In you, O LORD, do I take refuge;
    let me never be put to shame;
    in your righteousness deliver me!
2 Incline your ear to me;
    rescue me speedily!
Be a rock of refuge for me,
    a strong fortress to save me!

3 For you are my rock and my fortress;
    and for your name's sake you lead me and guide me;
4 you take me out of the net they have hidden for me,
    for you are my refuge.
5 Into your hand I commit my spirit;
    you have redeemed me, O LORD, faithful God.

6 I hate those who pay regard to worthless idols,
    but I trust in the LORD.
7 I will rejoice and be glad in your steadfast love,
    because you have seen my affliction;
    you have known the distress of my soul,
8 and you have not delivered me into the hand of the enemy;
    you have set my feet in a broad place.

Reflection

Sing
praises
to the LORD,
O you his saints,
and give thanks to his
holy name.
For his anger is but for
a moment,
and his favor is for
a lifetime.
Weeping may tarry for
the night, but joy
comes with
the morning.
Psalm 30:4-5

MARCH 5
~ Psalm 31:9-13

9   Be gracious to me, O LORD, for I am in distress;
        my eye is wasted from grief;
        my soul and my body also.

10   For my life is spent with sorrow,
        and my years with sighing;
        my strength fails because of my iniquity,
        and my bones waste away.

11   Because of all my adversaries I have become a reproach,
        especially to my neighbors,
    and an object of dread to my acquaintances;
        those who see me in the street flee from me.

12   I have been forgotten like one who is dead;
        I have become like a broken vessel.

13   For I hear the whispering of many—
        terror on every side!—
    as they scheme together against me,
        as they plot to take my life.

Reflection

_____

_____

_____

_____

_____

_____

MARCH 6
~ Psalm 31:14-20

14   But I trust in you, O LORD;
         I say, "You are my God."
15   My times are in your hand;
         rescue me from the hand of my enemies and from
            my persecutors!
16   Make your face shine on your servant;
         save me in your steadfast love!
17   O LORD, let me not be put to shame,
         for I call upon you;
      let the wicked be put to shame;
         let them go silently to Sheol.
18   Let the lying lips be mute,
         which speak insolently against the righteous
         in pride and contempt.

19   Oh, how abundant is your goodness,
         which you have stored up for those who fear you
      and worked for those who take refuge in you,
         in the sight of the children of mankind!
20   In the cover of your presence you hide them
         from the plots of men;
      you store them in your shelter
         from the strife of tongues.

Reflection

MARCH 7
~ Psalm 31:21-24

21   Blessed be the LORD,
       for he has wondrously shown his steadfast love to me
       when I was in a besieged city.
22   I had said in my alarm,
       " I am cut off from your sight."
       But you heard the voice of my pleas for mercy
       when I cried to you for help.

23   Love the LORD, all you his saints!
       The LORD preserves the faithful
       but abundantly repays the one who acts in pride.
24   Be strong, and let your heart take courage,
       all you who wait for the LORD!

Reflection

MARCH 8
~ Psalm 32:1-5

Blessed Are the Forgiven

A Maskil of David.

1 Blessed is the one whose transgression is forgiven,
  whose sin is covered.
2 Blessed is the man against whom the LORD counts no iniquity,
  and in whose spirit there is no deceit.

3 For when I kept silent, my bones wasted away
  through my groaning all day long.
4 For day and night your hand was heavy upon me;
  my strength was dried up as by the heat of summer.   *Selah*

5 I acknowledged my sin to you,
  and I did not cover my iniquity;
  I said, "I will confess my transgressions to the LORD,"
  and you forgave the iniquity of my sin.   *Selah*

Reflection

MARCH 9
~ Psalm 32:6-11

6   Therefore let everyone who is godly
    offer prayer to you at a time when you may be found;
surely in the rush of great waters,
    they shall not reach him.
7   You are a hiding place for me;
    you preserve me from trouble;
    you surround me with shouts of deliverance.   *Selah*

8   I will instruct you and teach you in the way you should go;
    I will counsel you with my eye upon you.
9   Be not like a horse or a mule, without understanding,
    which must be curbed with bit and bridle,
    or it will not stay near you.

10 Many are the sorrows of the wicked,
    but steadfast love surrounds the one who trusts in
        the LORD.
11 Be glad in the LORD, and rejoice, O righteous,
    and shout for joy, all you upright in heart!

Reflection

_____

_____

_____

_____

_____

MARCH 10
~ Psalm 33:1-5

The Steadfast Love of the Lord

1 Shout for joy in the LORD, O you righteous!
  Praise befits the upright.
2 Give thanks to the LORD with the lyre;
  make melody to him with the harp of ten strings!
3 Sing to him a new song;
  play skillfully on the strings, with loud shouts.

4 For the word of the LORD is upright,
  and all his work is done in faithfulness.
5 He loves righteousness and justice;
  the earth is full of the steadfast love of the LORD.

Reflection

MARCH 11
~ Psalm 33:6-12

6   By the word of the LORD the heavens were made,
      and by the breath of his mouth all their host.
7   He gathers the waters of the sea as a heap;
      he puts the deeps in storehouses.

8   Let all the earth fear the LORD;
      let all the inhabitants of the world stand in awe of him!
9   For he spoke, and it came to be;
      he commanded, and it stood firm.

10   The LORD brings the counsel of the nations to nothing;
      he frustrates the plans of the peoples.
11   The counsel of the LORD stands forever,
      the plans of his heart to all generations.
12   Blessed is the nation whose God is the LORD,
      the people whom he has chosen as his heritage!

Reflection

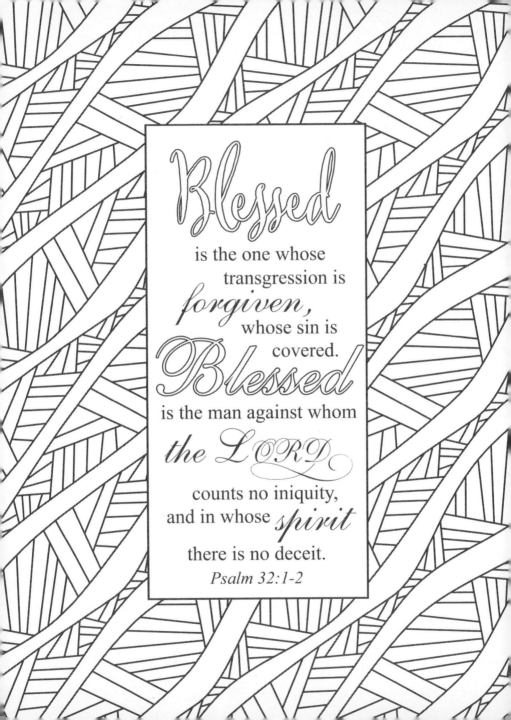

Blessed
is the one whose
transgression is
forgiven,
whose sin is
covered.
Blessed
is the man against whom
the LORD
counts no iniquity,
and in whose *spirit*
there is no deceit.
Psalm 32:1-2

MARCH 12
~ Psalm 33:13-17

13   The LORD looks down from heaven;
        he sees all the children of man;
14   from where he sits enthroned he looks out
        on all the inhabitants of the earth,
15   he who fashions the hearts of them all
        and observes all their deeds.
16   The king is not saved by his great army;
        a warrior is not delivered by his great strength.
17   The war horse is a false hope for salvation,
        and by its great might it cannot rescue.

Reflection

MARCH 13
~ Psalm 33:18-22

18   Behold, the eye of the LORD is on those who fear him,
         on those who hope in his steadfast love,
19   that he may deliver their soul from death
         and keep them alive in famine.

20   Our soul waits for the LORD;
         he is our help and our shield.
21   For our heart is glad in him,
         because we trust in his holy name.
22   Let your steadfast love, O LORD, be upon us,
         even as we hope in you.

Reflection

MARCH 14
~ Psalm 34:1-7

Taste and See That the *Lord Is Good*

Of David, when he changed his behavior before Abimelech, so that he drove him out, and he went away.

1   I will bless the LORD at all times;
      his praise shall continually be in my mouth.
2   My soul makes its boast in the LORD;
      let the humble hear and be glad.
3   Oh, magnify the LORD with me,
      and let us exalt his name together!

4   I sought the LORD, and he answered me
      and delivered me from all my fears.
5   Those who look to him are radiant,
      and their faces shall never be ashamed.
6   This poor man cried, and the LORD heard him
      and saved him out of all his troubles.
7   The angel of the LORD encamps
      around those who fear him, and delivers them.

Reflection

_____
_____
_____
_____
_____
_____

MARCH 15
~ Psalm 34:8-14

8   Oh, taste and see that the LORD is good!
        Blessed is the man who takes refuge in him!
9   Oh, fear the LORD, you his saints,
        for those who fear him have no lack!
10   The young lions suffer want and hunger;
        but those who seek the LORD lack no good thing.

11   Come, O children, listen to me;
        I will teach you the fear of the LORD.
12   What man is there who desires life
        and loves many days, that he may see good?
13   Keep your tongue from evil
        and your lips from speaking deceit.
14   Turn away from evil and do good;
        seek peace and pursue it.

Reflection

MARCH 16
~ Psalm 34:15-22

15   The eyes of the Lord are toward the righteous
       and his ears toward their cry.

16   The face of the Lord is against those who do evil,
       to cut off the memory of them from the earth.

17   When the righteous cry for help, the Lord hears
       and delivers them out of all their troubles.

18   The Lord is near to the brokenhearted
       and saves the crushed in spirit.

19   Many are the afflictions of the righteous,
       but the Lord delivers him out of them all.

20   He keeps all his bones;
       not one of them is broken.

21   Affliction will slay the wicked,
       and those who hate the righteous will be condemned.

22   The Lord redeems the life of his servants;
       none of those who take refuge in him will be condemned.

Reflection

MARCH 17
~ Psalm 35:1-6

Great Is the *Lord*

Of David.

1 Contend, O Lord, with those who contend with me;
   fight against those who fight against me!
2 Take hold of shield and buckler
   and rise for my help!
3 Draw the spear and javelin
   against my pursuers!
   Say to my soul,
   " I am your salvation!"

4 Let them be put to shame and dishonor
   who seek after my life!
   Let them be turned back and disappointed
   who devise evil against me!
5 Let them be like chaff before the wind,
   with the angel of the Lord driving them away!
6 Let their way be dark and slippery,
   with the angel of the Lord pursuing them!

Reflection

MARCH 18
~ Psalm 35:7-14

7   For without cause they hid their net for me;
        without cause they dug a pit for my life.
8   Let destruction come upon him when he does not know it!
     And let the net that he hid ensnare him;
        let him fall into it—to his destruction!

9   Then my soul will rejoice in the LORD,
        exulting in his salvation.
10   All my bones shall say,
        "O LORD, who is like you,
     delivering the poor
        from him who is too strong for him,
        the poor and needy from him who robs him?"

11   Malicious witnesses rise up;
        they ask me of things that I do not know.
12   They repay me evil for good;
        my soul is bereft.
13   But I, when they were sick—
        I wore sackcloth;
        I afflicted myself with fasting;
     I prayed with head bowed on my chest.
14   I went about as though I grieved for my friend
            or my brother;
     as one who laments his mother,
        I bowed down in mourning.

Reflection

Oh, taste and see that the LORD is good! Blessed is the man who takes refuge in him!

Psalm 34:8

MARCH 19
~ Psalm 35:15-21

15   But at my stumbling they rejoiced and gathered;
        they gathered together against me;
     wretches whom I did not know
        tore at me without ceasing;
16   like profane mockers at a feast,
        they gnash at me with their teeth.

17   How long, O Lord, will you look on?
        Rescue me from their destruction,
        my precious life from the lions!
18   I will thank you in the great congregation;
        in the mighty throng I will praise you.

19   Let not those rejoice over me
        who are wrongfully my foes,
     and let not those wink the eye
        who hate me without cause.
20   For they do not speak peace,
        but against those who are quiet in the land
        they devise words of deceit.
21   They open wide their mouths against me;
        they say, "Aha, Aha!
        Our eyes have seen it!"

Reflection

MARCH 20
~ Psalm 35:22-28

22   You have seen, O LORD; be not silent!
       O Lord, be not far from me!
23   Awake and rouse yourself for my vindication,
       for my cause, my God and my Lord!
24   Vindicate me, O LORD, my God,
       according to your righteousness,
       and let them not rejoice over me!
25   Let them not say in their hearts,
       "Aha, our heart's desire!"
    Let them not say, "We have swallowed him up."

26   Let them be put to shame and disappointed altogether
       who rejoice at my calamity!
    Let them be clothed with shame and dishonor
       who magnify themselves against me!

27   Let those who delight in my righteousness
       shout for joy and be glad
       and say evermore,
  "Great is the LORD,
       who delights in the welfare of his servant!"
28   Then my tongue shall tell of your righteousness
       and of your praise all the day long.

Reflection

MARCH 21
~ Psalm 36:1-6

How Precious Is Your Steadfast Love

To the choirmaster. Of David, the servant of the LORD.

1 Transgression speaks to the wicked
   deep in his heart;
there is no fear of God
   before his eyes.
2 For he flatters himself in his own eyes
   that his iniquity cannot be found out and hated.
3 The words of his mouth are trouble and deceit;
   he has ceased to act wisely and do good.
4 He plots trouble while on his bed;
   he sets himself in a way that is not good;
   he does not reject evil.

5 Your steadfast love, O LORD, extends to the heavens,
   your faithfulness to the clouds.
6 Your righteousness is like the mountains of God;
   your judgments are like the great deep;
   man and beast you save, O LORD.

Reflection

MARCH 22
~ Psalm 36:7-12

7 How precious is your steadfast love, O God!
   The children of mankind take refuge in the shadow of
   your wings.
8 They feast on the abundance of your house,
   and you give them drink from the river of your delights.
9 For with you is the fountain of life;
   in your light do we see light.

10 Oh, continue your steadfast love to those who know you,
    and your righteousness to the upright of heart!
11 Let not the foot of arrogance come upon me,
    nor the hand of the wicked drive me away.
12 There the evildoers lie fallen;
    they are thrust down, unable to rise.

Reflection

MARCH 23
~ Psalm 37:1-7

He Will Not Forsake *His Saints*

Of David.

1 Fret not yourself because of evildoers;
   be not envious of wrongdoers!
2 For they will soon fade like the grass
   and wither like the green herb.

3 Trust in the LORD, and do good;
   dwell in the land and befriend faithfulness.
4 Delight yourself in the LORD,
   and he will give you the desires of your heart.

5 Commit your way to the LORD;
   trust in him, and he will act.
6 He will bring forth your righteousness as the light,
   and your justice as the noonday.

7 Be still before the LORD and wait patiently for him;
   fret not yourself over the one who prospers in his way,
   over the man who carries out evil devices!

Reflection

MARCH 24
~ Psalm 37:8-13

8   Refrain from anger, and forsake wrath!
        Fret not yourself; it tends only to evil.
9   For the evildoers shall be cut off,
        but those who wait for the LORD shall inherit the land.

10   In just a little while, the wicked will be no more;
        though you look carefully at his place, he will not be there.
11   But the meek shall inherit the land
        and delight themselves in abundant peace.

12   The wicked plots against the righteous
        and gnashes his teeth at him,
13   but the Lord laughs at the wicked,
        for he sees that his day is coming.

Reflection

MARCH 25
~ Psalm 37:14-19

14   The wicked draw the sword and bend their bows
        to bring down the poor and needy,
        to slay those whose way is upright;
15   their sword shall enter their own heart,
        and their bows shall be broken.

16   Better is the little that the righteous has
        than the abundance of many wicked.
17   For the arms of the wicked shall be broken,
        but the LORD upholds the righteous.

18   The LORD knows the days of the blameless,
        and their heritage will remain forever;
19   they are not put to shame in evil times;
        in the days of famine they have abundance.

Reflection

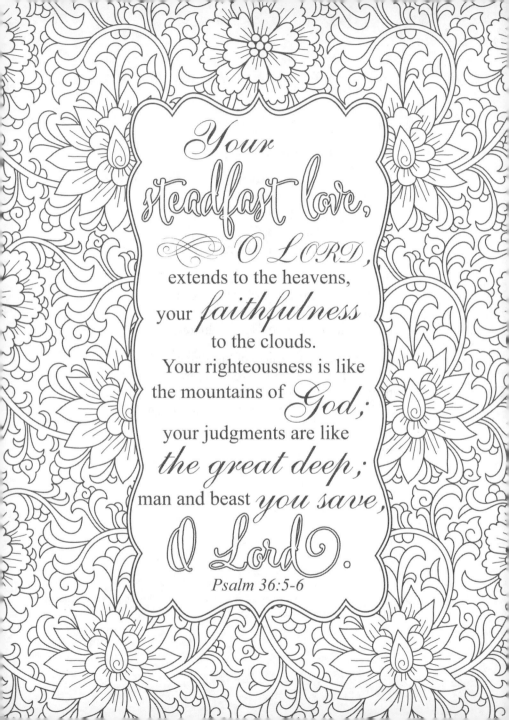

Your *steadfast love,* O LORD, extends to the heavens, your *faithfulness* to the clouds. Your righteousness is like the mountains of *God;* your judgments are like *the great deep;* man and beast *you save,* *O Lord.*

Psalm 36:5-6

MARCH 26
~ Psalm 37:20-26

20   But the wicked will perish;
        the enemies of the LORD are like the glory of the pastures;
        they vanish—like smoke they vanish away.

21   The wicked borrows but does not pay back,
        but the righteous is generous and gives;
22   for those blessed by the LORD shall inherit the land,
        but those cursed by him shall be cut off.

23   The steps of a man are established by the LORD,
        when he delights in his way;
24   though he fall, he shall not be cast headlong,
        for the LORD upholds his hand.

25   I have been young, and now am old,
        yet I have not seen the righteous forsaken
        or his children begging for bread.
26   He is ever lending generously,
        and his children become a blessing.

Reflection

MARCH 27
~ Psalm 37:27-34

27 Turn away from evil and do good;
     so shall you dwell forever.
28 For the LORD loves justice;
     he will not forsake his saints.
They are preserved forever,
     but the children of the wicked shall be cut off.
29 The righteous shall inherit the land
     and dwell upon it forever.

30 The mouth of the righteous utters wisdom,
     and his tongue speaks justice.
31 The law of his God is in his heart;
     his steps do not slip.

32 The wicked watches for the righteous
     and seeks to put him to death.
33 The LORD will not abandon him to his power
     or let him be condemned when he is brought to trial.

34 Wait for the LORD and keep his way,
     and he will exalt you to inherit the land;
     you will look on when the wicked are cut off.

Reflection

MARCH 28
~ Psalm 37:35-40

35   I have seen a wicked, ruthless man,
       spreading himself like a green laurel tree.
36   But he passed away, and behold, he was no more;
       though I sought him, he could not be found.

37   Mark the blameless and behold the upright,
       for there is a future for the man of peace.
38   But transgressors shall be altogether destroyed;
       the future of the wicked shall be cut off.

39   The salvation of the righteous is from the Lord;
       he is their stronghold in the time of trouble.
40   The Lord helps them and delivers them;
       he delivers them from the wicked and saves them,
       because they take refuge in him.

Reflection

MARCH 29
~ Psalm 38:1-8

Do Not *Forsake Me, O Lord*

A Psalm of David, for the memorial offering.

1   O LORD, rebuke me not in your anger,
         nor discipline me in your wrath!
2   For your arrows have sunk into me,
         and your hand has come down on me.

3   There is no soundness in my flesh
         because of your indignation;
     there is no health in my bones
         because of my sin.
4   For my iniquities have gone over my head;
         like a heavy burden, they are too heavy for me.

5   My wounds stink and fester
         because of my foolishness,
6   I am utterly bowed down and prostrate;
         all the day I go about mourning.
7   For my sides are filled with burning,
         and there is no soundness in my flesh.
8   I am feeble and crushed;
         I groan because of the tumult of my heart.

Reflection

MARCH 30
~ Psalm 38:9-16

9   O Lord, all my longing is before you;
       my sighing is not hidden from you.

10   My heart throbs; my strength fails me,
       and the light of my eyes—it also has gone from me.

11   My friends and companions stand aloof from my plague,
       and my nearest kin stand far off.

12   Those who seek my life lay their snares;
       those who seek my hurt speak of ruin
       and meditate treachery all day long.

13   But I am like a deaf man; I do not hear,
       like a mute man who does not open his mouth.

14   I have become like a man who does not hear,
       and in whose mouth are no rebukes.

15   But for you, O Lord, do I wait;
       it is you, O Lord my God, who will answer.

16   For I said, "Only let them not rejoice over me,
       who boast against me when my foot slips!"

Reflection

MARCH 31
~ Psalm 38:17-22

17   For I am ready to fall,
        and my pain is ever before me.

18   I confess my iniquity;
        I am sorry for my sin.

19   But my foes are vigorous, they are mighty,
        and many are those who hate me wrongfully.

20   Those who render me evil for good
        accuse me because I follow after good.

21   Do not forsake me, O Lord!
        O my God, be not far from me!

22   Make haste to help me,
        O Lord, my salvation!

Reflection

APRIL 1
~ Psalm 39:1-6

What Is the *Measure* of *My Days?*

To the choirmaster: to Jeduthun. A Psalm of David.

1. I said, "I will guard my ways,
   that I may not sin with my tongue;
   I will guard my mouth with a muzzle,
   so long as the wicked are in my presence."
2. I was mute and silent;
   I held my peace to no avail,
   and my distress grew worse.
3. My heart became hot within me.
   As I mused, the fire burned;
   then I spoke with my tongue:

4. "O LORD, make me know my end
   and what is the measure of my days;
   let me know how fleeting I am!
5. Behold, you have made my days a few handbreadths,
   and my lifetime is as nothing before you.
   Surely all mankind stands as a mere breath!   *Selah*
6. Surely a man goes about as a shadow!
   Surely for nothing they are in turmoil;
   man heaps up wealth and does not know who will gather!

Reflection

The salvation of the **righteous** is from the LORD; he is their **stronghold** in the time of trouble.

Psalm 37:39

APRIL 2
~ Psalm 39:7-13

7 " And now, O Lord, for what do I wait?
    My hope is in you.
8 Deliver me from all my transgressions.
    Do not make me the scorn of the fool!
9 I am mute; I do not open my mouth,
    for it is you who have done it.
10 Remove your stroke from me;
    I am spent by the hostility of your hand.
11 When you discipline a man
    with rebukes for sin,
   you consume like a moth what is dear to him;
    surely all mankind is a mere breath!   *Selah*

12 " Hear my prayer, O LORD,
    and give ear to my cry;
    hold not your peace at my tears!
   For I am a sojourner with you,
    a guest, like all my fathers.
13 Look away from me, that I may smile again,
    before I depart and am no more!"

Reflection

APRIL 3
~ Psalm 40:1-5

My Help and My *Deliverer*

To the choirmaster. A Psalm of David.

1 I waited patiently for the LORD;
 he inclined to me and heard my cry.
2 He drew me up from the pit of destruction,
 out of the miry bog,
and set my feet upon a rock,
 making my steps secure.
3 He put a new song in my mouth,
 a song of praise to our God.
Many will see and fear,
 and put their trust in the LORD.

4 Blessed is the man who makes
 the LORD his trust,
who does not turn to the proud,
 to those who go astray after a lie!
5 You have multiplied, O LORD my God,
 your wondrous deeds and your thoughts toward us;
 none can compare with you!
I will proclaim and tell of them,
 yet they are more than can be told.

Reflection

APRIL 4
~ Psalm 40:6-10

6   In sacrifice and offering you have not delighted,
        but you have given me an open ear.
    Burnt offering and sin offering
        you have not required.

7   Then I said, "Behold, I have come;
        in the scroll of the book it is written of me:

8   I delight to do your will, O my God;
        your law is within my heart."

9   I have told the glad news of deliverance
        in the great congregation;
    behold, I have not restrained my lips,
        as you know, O Lord.

10   I have not hidden your deliverance within my heart;
        I have spoken of your faithfulness and your salvation;
    I have not concealed your steadfast love and your faithfulness
        from the great congregation.

Reflection

APRIL 5
~ Psalm 40:11-17

11 As for you, O LORD, you will not restrain
    your mercy from me;
   your steadfast love and your faithfulness will
    ever preserve me!
12 For evils have encompassed me
    beyond number;
   my iniquities have overtaken me,
    and I cannot see;
   they are more than the hairs of my head;
    my heart fails me.

13 Be pleased, O LORD, to deliver me!
    O LORD, make haste to help me!
14 Let those be put to shame and disappointed altogether
    who seek to snatch away my life;
   let those be turned back and brought to dishonor
    who delight in my hurt!
15 Let those be appalled because of their shame
    who say to me, "Aha, Aha!"

16 But may all who seek you
    rejoice and be glad in you;
   may those who love your salvation
    say continually, "Great is the LORD!"
17 As for me, I am poor and needy,
    but the Lord takes thought for me.
   You are my help and my deliverer;
    do not delay, O my God!

Reflection

APRIL 6
~ Psalm 41:1-7

O LORD, Be Gracious to Me

To the choirmaster. A Psalm of David.

1 Blessed is the one who considers the poor!
   In the day of trouble the LORD delivers him;
2 the LORD protects him and keeps him alive;
   he is called blessed in the land;
   you do not give him up to the will of his enemies.
3 The LORD sustains him on his sickbed;
   in his illness you restore him to full health.

4 As for me, I said, "O LORD, be gracious to me;
   heal me, for I have sinned against you!"
5 My enemies say of me in malice,
   "When will he die, and his name perish?"
6 And when one comes to see me, he utters empty words,
   while his heart gathers iniquity;
   when he goes out, he tells it abroad.
7 All who hate me whisper together about me;
   they imagine the worst for me.

Reflection

APRIL 7
~ Psalm 41:8-13

8   They say, "A deadly thing is poured out on him;
       he will not rise again from where he lies."

9   Even my close friend in whom I trusted,
       who ate my bread, has lifted his heel against me.

10   But you, O Lord, be gracious to me,
       and raise me up, that I may repay them!

11   By this I know that you delight in me:
       my enemy will not shout in triumph over me.

12   But you have upheld me because of my integrity,
       and set me in your presence forever.

13   Blessed be the Lord, the God of Israel,
       from everlasting to everlasting!
              Amen and Amen.

Reflection

APRIL 8
~ Psalm 42:1-6

Why Are You Cast Down, O My Soul?

To the choirmaster. A Maskil of the Sons of Korah.

1   As a deer pants for flowing streams,
       so pants my soul for you, O God.
2   My soul thirsts for God,
       for the living God.
    When shall I come and appear before God?
3   My tears have been my food
       day and night,
    while they say to me all the day long,
       "Where is your God?"
4   These things I remember,
       as I pour out my soul:
    how I would go with the throng
       and lead them in procession to the house of God
    with glad shouts and songs of praise,
       a multitude keeping festival.

5   Why are you cast down, O my soul,
       and why are you in turmoil within me?
    Hope in God; for I shall again praise him,
6   my salvation and my God.

    My soul is cast down within me;
       therefore I remember you
    from the land of Jordan and of Hermon,
       from Mount Mizar.

As a *deer* pants for *flowing streams,* so pants my soul for you, *O God.* My soul thirsts *for God,* for the *living God.* When shall I come & appear before God?
Psalm 42:1-2

APRIL 9
~ Psalm 42:7-11

7   Deep calls to deep
      at the roar of your waterfalls;
    all your breakers and your waves
      have gone over me.

8   By day the Lord commands his steadfast love,
      and at night his song is with me,
      a prayer to the God of my life.

9   I say to God, my rock:
      "Why have you forgotten me?
    Why do I go mourning
      because of the oppression of the enemy?"

10   As with a deadly wound in my bones,
      my adversaries taunt me,
    while they say to me all the day long,
      "Where is your God?"

11   Why are you cast down, O my soul,
      and why are you in turmoil within me?
    Hope in God; for I shall again praise him,
      my salvation and my God.

Reflection

APRIL 10
~ Psalm 43

Send Out *Your Light & Your Truth*

1   Vindicate me, O God, and defend my cause
       against an ungodly people,
from the deceitful and unjust man
       deliver me!

2   For you are the God in whom I take refuge;
       why have you rejected me?
Why do I go about mourning
       because of the oppression of the enemy?

3   Send out your light and your truth;
       let them lead me;
let them bring me to your holy hill
       and to your dwelling!

4   Then I will go to the altar of God,
       to God my exceeding joy,
and I will praise you with the lyre,
       O God, my God.

5   Why are you cast down, O my soul,
       and why are you in turmoil within me?
Hope in God; for I shall again praise him,
       my salvation and my God.

Reflection

APRIL 11
~ Psalm 44:1-6

Come to Our Helper

To the choirmaster. A Maskil of the Sons of Korah.

1   O God, we have heard with our ears,
     our fathers have told us,
what deeds you performed in their days,
     in the days of old:
2   you with your own hand drove out the nations,
     but them you planted;
you afflicted the peoples,
     but them you set free;
3   for not by their own sword did they win the land,
     nor did their own arm save them,
but your right hand and your arm,
     and the light of your face,
     for you delighted in them.

4   You are my King, O God;
     ordain salvation for Jacob!
5   Through you we push down our foes;
     through your name we tread down those who rise up
       against us.
6   For not in my bow do I trust,
     nor can my sword save me.

Reflection

APRIL 12
~ Psalm 44:7-12

7   But you have saved us from our foes
      and have put to shame those who hate us.
8   In God we have boasted continually,
      and we will give thanks to your name forever.   *Selah*

9   But you have rejected us and disgraced us
      and have not gone out with our armies.
10 You have made us turn back from the foe,
      and those who hate us have gotten spoil.
11 You have made us like sheep for slaughter
      and have scattered us among the nations.
12 You have sold your people for a trifle,
      demanding no high price for them.

Reflection

APRIL 13
~ Psalm 44:13-19

13   You have made us the taunt of our neighbors,
        the derision and scorn of those around us.

14   You have made us a byword among the nations,
        a laughingstock among the peoples.

15   All day long my disgrace is before me,
        and shame has covered my face

16   at the sound of the taunter and reviler,
        at the sight of the enemy and the avenger.

17   All this has come upon us,
        though we have not forgotten you,
        and we have not been false to your covenant.

18   Our heart has not turned back,
        nor have our steps departed from your way;

19   yet you have broken us in the place of jackals
        and covered us with the shadow of death.

Reflection

APRIL 14
~ Psalm 44:20-26

20 If we had forgotten the name of our God
   or spread out our hands to a foreign god,
21 would not God discover this?
   For he knows the secrets of the heart.
22 Yet for your sake we are killed all the day long;
   we are regarded as sheep to be slaughtered.

23 Awake! Why are you sleeping, O Lord?
   Rouse yourself! Do not reject us forever!
24 Why do you hide your face?
   Why do you forget our affliction and oppression?
25 For our soul is bowed down to the dust;
   our belly clings to the ground.
26 Rise up; come to our help!
   Redeem us for the sake of your steadfast love!

Reflection

APRIL 15
~ Psalm 45:1-8a

Your Throne, O God, Is Forever

To the choirmaster: according to Lilies. A Maskil of the Sons of Korah; a love song.

1   My heart overflows with a pleasing theme;
      I address my verses to the king;
      my tongue is like the pen of a ready scribe.

2   You are the most handsome of the sons of men;
      grace is poured upon your lips;
      therefore God has blessed you forever.

3   Gird your sword on your thigh, O mighty one,
      in your splendor and majesty!

4   In your majesty ride out victoriously
      for the cause of truth and meekness and righteousness;
      let your right hand teach you awesome deeds!

5   Your arrows are sharp
      in the heart of the king's enemies;
      the peoples fall under you.

6   Your throne, O God, is forever and ever.
      The scepter of your kingdom is a scepter of uprightness;

7   you have loved righteousness and hated wickedness.
   Therefore God, your God, has anointed you
      with the oil of gladness beyond your companions;

8   your robes are all fragrant with myrrh and aloes
      and cassia.

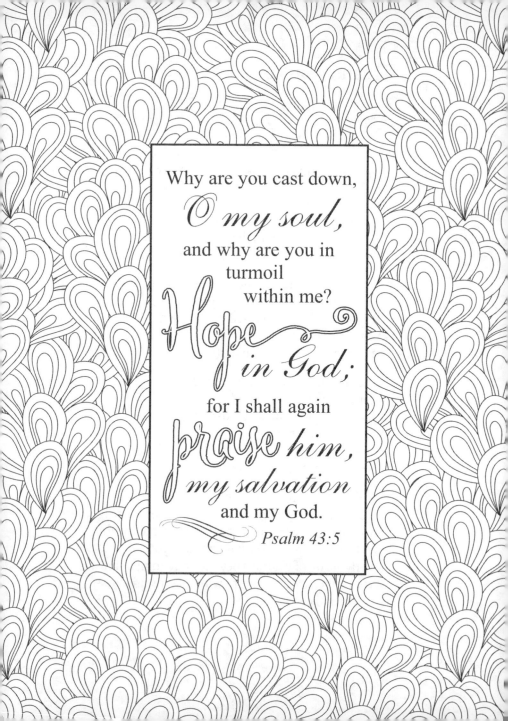

Why are you cast down,
O my soul,
and why are you in
turmoil
within me?
Hope
in God;
for I shall again
praise him,
my salvation
and my God.
Psalm 43:5

APRIL 16
~ Psalm 45:8b-17

From ivory palaces stringed instruments make you glad;
9   daughters of kings are among your ladies of honor;
at your right hand stands the queen in gold of Ophir.

10   Hear, O daughter, and consider, and incline your ear:
forget your people and your father's house,
11   and the king will desire your beauty.
Since he is your lord, bow to him.
12   The people of Tyre will seek your favor with gifts,
the richest of the people.

13   All glorious is the princess in her chamber, with robes
interwoven with gold.
14   In many-colored robes she is led to the king,
with her virgin companions following behind her.
15   With joy and gladness they are led along
as they enter the palace of the king.

16   In place of your fathers shall be your sons;
you will make them princes in all the earth.
17   I will cause your name to be remembered in all generations;
therefore nations will praise you forever and ever.

Reflection

APRIL 17
~ Psalm 46:1-5

God Is Our

To the choirmaster. Of the Sons of Korah. According to Alamoth. A Song.

1   God is our refuge and strength,
     a very present help in trouble.
2   Therefore we will not fear though the earth gives way,
     though the mountains be moved into the heart of the sea,
3   though its waters roar and foam,
     though the mountains tremble at its swelling.   *Selah*

4   There is a river whose streams make glad the city of God,
     the holy habitation of the Most High.
5   God is in the midst of her; she shall not be moved;
     God will help her when morning dawns.

Reflection

APRIL 18
~ Psalm 46:6-11

6   The nations rage, the kingdoms totter;
    he utters his voice, the earth melts.
7   The LORD of hosts is with us;
    the God of Jacob is our fortress.   *Selah*

8   Come, behold the works of the LORD,
    how he has brought desolations on the earth.
9   He makes wars cease to the end of the earth;
    he breaks the bow and shatters the spear;
    he burns the chariots with fire.
10 " Be still, and know that I am God.
    I will be exalted among the nations,
    I will be exalted in the earth!"
11 The LORD of hosts is with us;
    the God of Jacob is our fortress.   *Selah*

Reflection

APRIL 19
~ Psalm 47:1-4

God Is King over All the Earth

To the choirmaster. A Psalm of the Sons of Korah.

1 Clap your hands, all peoples!
   Shout to God with loud songs of joy!
2 For the LORD, the Most High, is to be feared,
   a great king over all the earth.
3 He subdued peoples under us,
   and nations under our feet.
4 He chose our heritage for us,
   the pride of Jacob whom he loves. *Selah*

Reflection

_____
_____
_____
_____
_____
_____
_____
_____
_____
_____
_____

APRIL 20
~ Psalm 47:5-9

5   God has gone up with a shout,
        the LORD with the sound of a trumpet.

6   Sing praises to God, sing praises!
        Sing praises to our King, sing praises!

7   For God is the King of all the earth;
        sing praises with a psalm!

8   God reigns over the nations;
        God sits on his holy throne.

9   The princes of the peoples gather
        as the people of the God of Abraham.
    For the shields of the earth belong to God;
        he is highly exalted!

Reflection

APRIL 21
~ Psalm 48:1-8

Zion, the City of *Our God*

A Song. A Psalm of the Sons of Korah.

1 Great is the LORD and greatly to be praised
   in the city of our God!
2 His holy mountain, beautiful in elevation,
   is the joy of all the earth,
   Mount Zion, in the far north,
   the city of the great King.
3 Within her citadels God
   has made himself known as a fortress.

4 For behold, the kings assembled;
   they came on together.
5 As soon as they saw it, they were astounded;
   they were in panic; they took to flight.
6 Trembling took hold of them there,
   anguish as of a woman in labor.
7 By the east wind you shattered
   the ships of Tarshish.
8 As we have heard, so have we seen
   in the city of the LORD of hosts,
   in the city of our God,
   which God will establish forever.   *Selah*

Reflection

APRIL 22
~ Psalm 48:9-14

9 We have thought on your steadfast love, O God,
   in the midst of your temple.
10 As your name, O God,
   so your praise reaches to the ends of the earth.
   Your right hand is filled with righteousness.
11   Let Mount Zion be glad!
   Let the daughters of Judah rejoice
   because of your judgments!

12 Walk about Zion, go around her,
   number her towers,
13 consider well her ramparts,
   go through her citadels,
   that you may tell the next generation
14   that this is God,
   our God forever and ever.
   He will guide us forever.

Reflection

"Be still, and know that I am God. I will be exalted among the nations, I will be exalted in the earth!"

Psalm 46:10

APRIL 23
~ Psalm 49:1-6

 Should I Fear *in Times* of Trouble?

To the choirmaster. A Psalm of the Sons of Korah.

1   Hear this, all peoples!
      Give ear, all inhabitants of the world,
2   both low and high,
      rich and poor together!
3   My mouth shall speak wisdom;
      the meditation of my heart shall be understanding.
4   I will incline my ear to a proverb;
      I will solve my riddle to the music of the lyre.

5   Why should I fear in times of trouble,
      when the iniquity of those who cheat me surrounds me,
6   those who trust in their wealth
      and boast of the abundance of their riches?

Reflection

APRIL 24
~ Psalm 49:7-13

7   Truly no man can ransom another,
    or give to God the price of his life,
8   for the ransom of their life is costly
    and can never suffice,
9   that he should live on forever
    and never see the pit.

10 For he sees that even the wise die;
    the fool and the stupid alike must perish
    and leave their wealth to others.
11 Their graves are their homes forever,
    their dwelling places to all generations,
    though they called lands by their own names.
12 Man in his pomp will not remain;
    he is like the beasts that perish.

13 This is the path of those who have foolish confidence;
    yet after them people approve of their boasts.

Selah

Reflection

_____
_____
_____
_____
_____
_____
_____
_____
_____

APRIL 25
~ Psalm 49:14-20

14   Like sheep they are appointed for Sheol;
        death shall be their shepherd,
    and the upright shall rule over them in the morning.
        Their form shall be consumed in Sheol, with no place
        to dwell.

15   But God will ransom my soul from the power of Sheol,
        for he will receive me.   *Selah*

16   Be not afraid when a man becomes rich,
        when the glory of his house increases.

17   For when he dies he will carry nothing away;
        his glory will not go down after him.

18   For though, while he lives, he counts himself blessed
        —and though you get praise when you do well for
        yourself—

19   his soul will go to the generation of his fathers,
        who will never again see light.

20   Man in his pomp yet without understanding is like the beasts
        that perish.

Reflection

APRIL 26
~ Psalm 50:1-6

God Himself Is Judge

A Psalm of Asaph.

1 The Mighty One, God the LORD,
    speaks and summons the earth
    from the rising of the sun to its setting.
2 Out of Zion, the perfection of beauty,
    God shines forth.

3 Our God comes; he does not keep silence;
    before him is a devouring fire,
    around him a mighty tempest.
4 He calls to the heavens above
    and to the earth, that he may judge his people:
5 "Gather to me my faithful ones,
    who made a covenant with me by sacrifice!"
6 The heavens declare his righteousness,
    for God himself is judge!   *Selah*

Reflection

APRIL 27
~ Psalm 50:7-11

7   " Hear, O my people, and I will speak;
        O Israel, I will testify against you.
        I am God, your God.
8   Not for your sacrifices do I rebuke you;
        your burnt offerings are continually before me.
9   I will not accept a bull from your house
        or goats from your folds.
10   For every beast of the forest is mine,
        the cattle on a thousand hills.
11   I know all the birds of the hills,
        and all that moves in the field is mine.

Reflection

APRIL 28
~ Psalm 50:12-18

12   " If I were hungry, I would not tell you,
       for the world and its fullness are mine.
13   Do I eat the flesh of bulls
       or drink the blood of goats?
14   Offer to God a sacrifice of thanksgiving,
       and perform your vows to the Most High,
15   and call upon me in the day of trouble;
       I will deliver you, and you shall glorify me."

16   But to the wicked God says:
       " What right have you to recite my statutes
       or take my covenant on your lips?
17   For you hate discipline,
       and you cast my words behind you.
18   If you see a thief, you are pleased with him,
       and you keep company with adulterers.

Reflection

APRIL 29
~ Psalm 50:19-23

19   "You give your mouth free rein for evil,
     and your tongue frames deceit.
20   You sit and speak against your brother;
     you slander your own mother's son.
21   These things you have done, and I have been silent;
     you thought that I was one like yourself.
     But now I rebuke you and lay the charge before you.

22   "Mark this, then, you who forget God,
     lest I tear you apart, and there be none to deliver!
23   The one who offers thanksgiving as his sacrifice glorifies me;
     to one who orders his way rightly
     I will show the salvation of God!"

Reflection

The
Mighty One, God the Lord,
speaks and summons the earth
from the rising of the *sun* to its setting.
Out of Zion, *the perfection of beauty,*
God shines forth. Psalm 50:1-2

APRIL 30
~ Psalm 51:1-6

Create in Me *a Clean Heart, O God*

To the choirmaster. A Psalm of David, when Nathan the prophet went to him, after he had gone in to Bathsheba.

1   Have mercy on me, O God,
       according to your steadfast love;
    according to your abundant mercy
       blot out my transgressions.
2   Wash me thoroughly from my iniquity,
       and cleanse me from my sin!

3   For I know my transgressions,
       and my sin is ever before me.
4   Against you, you only, have I sinned
       and done what is evil in your sight,
    so that you may be justified in your words
       and blameless in your judgment.
5   Behold, I was brought forth in iniquity,
       and in sin did my mother conceive me.
6   Behold, you delight in truth in the inward being,
       and you teach me wisdom in the secret heart.

Reflection

MAY 1
~ Psalm 51:7-12

7   Purge me with hyssop, and I shall be clean;
       wash me, and I shall be whiter than snow.

8   Let me hear joy and gladness;
       let the bones that you have broken rejoice.

9   Hide your face from my sins,
       and blot out all my iniquities.

10   Create in me a clean heart, O God,
       and renew a right spirit within me.

11   Cast me not away from your presence,
       and take not your Holy Spirit from me.

12   Restore to me the joy of your salvation,
       and uphold me with a willing spirit.

Reflection

MAY 2
~ Psalm 51:13-19

13   Then I will teach transgressors your ways,
        and sinners will return to you.

14   Deliver me from bloodguiltiness, O God,
        O God of my salvation,
        and my tongue will sing aloud of your righteousness.

15   O Lord, open my lips,
        and my mouth will declare your praise.

16   For you will not delight in sacrifice, or I would give it;
        you will not be pleased with a burnt offering.

17   The sacrifices of God are a broken spirit;
        a broken and contrite heart, O God, you will not despise.

18   Do good to Zion in your good pleasure;
        build up the walls of Jerusalem;

19   then will you delight in right sacrifices,
        in burnt offerings and whole burnt offerings;
        then bulls will be offered on your altar.

Reflection

MAY 3
~ Psalm 52:1-5

The Steadfast Love of God Endures

To the choirmaster. A Maskil of David, when Doeg, the Edomite, came and told Saul, "David has come to the house of Ahimelech."

1 Why do you boast of evil, O mighty man?
    The steadfast love of God endures all the day.
2 Your tongue plots destruction,
    like a sharp razor, you worker of deceit.
3 You love evil more than good,
    and lying more than speaking what is right.   *Selah*
4 You love all words that devour,
    O deceitful tongue.

5 But God will break you down forever;
    he will snatch and tear you from your tent;
    he will uproot you from the land of the living.   *Selah*

Reflection

_____
_____
_____
_____
_____
_____
_____
_____
_____
_____
_____
_____
_____

MAY 4
~ Psalm 52:6-9

6   The righteous shall see and fear,
        and shall laugh at him, saying,
7   " See the man who would not make
        God his refuge,
    but trusted in the abundance of his riches
        and sought refuge in his own destruction!"

8   But I am like a green olive tree
        in the house of God.
    I trust in the steadfast love of God
        forever and ever.
9   I will thank you forever,
        because you have done it.
    I will wait for your name, for it is good,
        in the presence of the godly.

Reflection

MAY 5
~ Psalm 53

There Is None Who Does Good

To the choirmaster: according to Mahalath. A Maskil of David.

1   The fool says in his heart, "There is no God."
  They are corrupt, doing abominable iniquity;
  there is none who does good.

2   God looks down from heaven
  on the children of man
 to see if there are any who understand,
  who seek after God.

3   They have all fallen away;
  together they have become corrupt;
 there is none who does good,
  not even one.

4   Have those who work evil no knowledge,
  who eat up my people as they eat bread,
  and do not call upon God?

5   There they are, in great terror,
  where there is no terror!
 For God scatters the bones of him who encamps against you;
  you put them to shame, for God has rejected them.

6   Oh, that salvation for Israel would come out of Zion!
  When God restores the fortunes of his people,
  let Jacob rejoice, let Israel be glad.

MAY 6
~ Psalm 54

The Lord Upholds My Life

To the choirmaster: with stringed instruments. A Maskil of David, when the Ziphites went and told Saul, "Is not David hiding among us?"

1   O God, save me by your name,
      and vindicate me by your might.
2   O God, hear my prayer;
      give ear to the words of my mouth.

3   For strangers have risen against me;
      ruthless men seek my life;
      they do not set God before themselves.   *Selah*

4   Behold, God is my helper;
      the Lord is the upholder of my life.
5   He will return the evil to my enemies;
      in your faithfulness put an end to them.

6   With a freewill offering I will sacrifice to you;
      I will give thanks to your name, O LORD, for it is good.
7   For he has delivered me from every trouble,
      and my eye has looked in triumph on my enemies.

Reflection

Create in me a clean heart, O God, & renew a right spirit within me. *Psalm 51:10*

MAY 7
~ Psalm 55:1-8

Cast Your Burden on the Lord

To the choirmaster: with stringed instruments. A Maskil of David.

1 Give ear to my prayer, O God,
   and hide not yourself from my plea for mercy!
2 Attend to me, and answer me;
   I am restless in my complaint and I moan,
3 because of the noise of the enemy,
   because of the oppression of the wicked.
   For they drop trouble upon me,
   and in anger they bear a grudge against me.

4 My heart is in anguish within me;
   the terrors of death have fallen upon me.
5 Fear and trembling come upon me,
   and horror overwhelms me.
6 And I say, "Oh, that I had wings like a dove!
   I would fly away and be at rest;
7 yes, I would wander far away;
   I would lodge in the wilderness;   *Selah*
8 I would hurry to find a shelter
   from the raging wind and tempest."

Reflection

MAY 8
~ Psalm 55:9-15

9   Destroy, O Lord, divide their tongues;
    for I see violence and strife in the city.
10 Day and night they go around it
    on its walls,
and iniquity and trouble are within it;
11   ruin is in its midst;
oppression and fraud
    do not depart from its marketplace.

12 For it is not an enemy who taunts me—
    then I could bear it;
it is not an adversary who deals insolently with me—
    then I could hide from him.
13 But it is you, a man, my equal,
    my companion, my familiar friend.
14 We used to take sweet counsel together;
    within God's house we walked in the throng.
15 Let death steal over them;
    let them go down to Sheol alive;
    for evil is in their dwelling place and in their heart.

Reflection

MAY 9
~ Psalm 55:16-23

16   But I call to God,
      and the LORD will save me.
17   Evening and morning and at noon
      I utter my complaint and moan,
      and he hears my voice.
18   He redeems my soul in safety
      from the battle that I wage,
      for many are arrayed against me.
19   God will give ear and humble them,
      he who is enthroned from of old,   *Selah*
      because they do not change
      and do not fear God.

20   My companion stretched out his hand against his friends;
      he violated his covenant.
21   His speech was smooth as butter,
      yet war was in his heart;
      his words were softer than oil,
      yet they were drawn swords.

22   Cast your burden on the LORD,
      and he will sustain you;
      he will never permit
      the righteous to be moved.

23   But you, O God, will cast them down
      into the pit of destruction;
      men of blood and treachery
      shall not live out half their days.
      But I will trust in you.

MAY 10
~ Psalm 56:1-7

In God I Trust

To the choirmaster: according to The Dove on Far-off Terebinths. A Miktam of David, when the Philistines seized him in Gath.

1 Be gracious to me, O God, for man tramples on me;
    all day long an attacker oppresses me;
2 my enemies trample on me all day long,
    for many attack me proudly.
3 When I am afraid,
    I put my trust in you.
4 In God, whose word I praise,
    in God I trust; I shall not be afraid.
    What can flesh do to me?

5 All day long they injure my cause;
    all their thoughts are against me for evil.
6 They stir up strife, they lurk;
    they watch my steps,
    as they have waited for my life.
7 For their crime will they escape?
    In wrath cast down the peoples, O God!

Reflection

MAY 11
~ Psalm 56:8-13

8   You have kept count of my tossings;
        put my tears in your bottle.
        Are they not in your book?

9   Then my enemies will turn back
        in the day when I call.
        This I know, that God is for me.

10   In God, whose word I praise,
        in the Lord, whose word I praise,

11   in God I trust; I shall not be afraid.
        What can man do to me?

12   I must perform my vows to you, O God;
        I will render thank offerings to you.

13   For you have delivered my soul from death,
        yes, my feet from falling,
      that I may walk before God
        in the light of life.

Reflection

MAY 12
~ Psalm 57:1-5

 Be over All *the Earth*

To the choirmaster: according to Do Not Destroy. A Miktam of David, when he fled from Saul, in the cave.

1 Be merciful to me, O God, be merciful to me,
   for in you my soul takes refuge;
in the shadow of your wings I will take refuge,
   till the storms of destruction pass by.
2 I cry out to God Most High,
   to God who fulfills his purpose for me.
3 He will send from heaven and save me;
   he will put to shame him who tramples on me.　　*Selah*
God will send out his steadfast love and his faithfulness!

4 My soul is in the midst of lions;
   I lie down amid fiery beasts—
the children of man, whose teeth are spears and arrows,
   whose tongues are sharp swords.

5 Be exalted, O God, above the heavens!
   Let your glory be over all the earth!

Reflection

MAY 13
~ Psalm 57:6-11

6   They set a net for my steps;
       my soul was bowed down.
    They dug a pit in my way,
       but they have fallen into it themselves.   *Selah*

7   My heart is steadfast, O God,
       my heart is steadfast!
    I will sing and make melody!

8   Awake, my glory!
    Awake, O harp and lyre!
      I will awake the dawn!

9   I will give thanks to you, O Lord, among the peoples;
      I will sing praises to you among the nations.

10   For your steadfast love is great to the heavens,
      your faithfulness to the clouds.

11   Be exalted, O God, above the heavens!
    Let your glory be over all the earth!

Reflection

When I am afraid,
I put my *trust in you.*
In God, whose word
I praise,
in God I trust;
I shall not be afraid.
What can flesh do to me?

Psalm 56:3-4

MAY 14
~ Psalm 58:1-5

God Who Judges *the Earth*

To the choirmaster: according to Do Not Destroy. A Miktam of David.

1   Do you indeed decree what is right, you gods?
     Do you judge the children of man uprightly?
2   No, in your hearts you devise wrongs;
     your hands deal out violence on earth.

3   The wicked are estranged from the womb;
     they go astray from birth, speaking lies.
4   They have venom like the venom of a serpent,
     like the deaf adder that stops its ear,
5   so that it does not hear the voice of charmers
     or of the cunning enchanter.

Reflection

MAY 15
~ Psalm 58:6-11

6   O God, break the teeth in their mouths;
        tear out the fangs of the young lions, O LORD!

7   Let them vanish like water that runs away;
        when he aims his arrows, let them be blunted.

8   Let them be like the snail that dissolves into slime,
        like the stillborn child who never sees the sun.

9   Sooner than your pots can feel the heat of thorns,
        whether green or ablaze, may he sweep them away!

10   The righteous will rejoice when he sees the vengeance;
        he will bathe his feet in the blood of the wicked.

11   Mankind will say, "Surely there is a reward for the righteous;
        surely there is a God who judges on earth."

Reflection

MAY 16
~ Psalm 59:1-7

 Deliver Me from My Enemies

To the choirmaster: according to Do Not Destroy. A Miktam of David, when Saul sent men to watch his house in order to kill him.

1 Deliver me from my enemies, O my God;
    protect me from those who rise up against me;
2 deliver me from those who work evil,
    and save me from bloodthirsty men.

3 For behold, they lie in wait for my life;
    fierce men stir up strife against me.
For no transgression or sin of mine, O LORD,
4   for no fault of mine, they run and make ready.
Awake, come to meet me, and see!
5   You, LORD God of hosts, are God of Israel.
Rouse yourself to punish all the nations;
    spare none of those who treacherously plot evil.   *Selah*

6 Each evening they come back,
    howling like dogs
    and prowling about the city.
7 There they are, bellowing with their mouths
    with swords in their lips—
    for "Who," they think, "will hear us?"

Reflection

_____
_____
_____
_____

MAY 17
~ Psalm 59:8-17

8 But you, O LORD, laugh at them;
     you hold all the nations in derision.
9 O my Strength, I will watch for you,
     for you, O God, are my fortress.
10 My God in his steadfast love will meet me;
     God will let me look in triumph on my enemies.

11 Kill them not, lest my people forget;
     make them totter by your power and bring them down,
     O Lord, our shield!
12 For the sin of their mouths, the words of their lips,
     let them be trapped in their pride.
   For the cursing and lies that they utter,
13   consume them in wrath;
     consume them till they are no more,
   that they may know that God rules over Jacob
     to the ends of the earth.   *Selah*

14 Each evening they come back,
     howling like dogs
     and prowling about the city.
15 They wander about for food
     and growl if they do not get their fill.

16 But I will sing of your strength;
     I will sing aloud of your steadfast love in the morning.
   For you have been to me a fortress
     and a refuge in the day of my distress.
17 O my Strength, I will sing praises to you,
     for you, O God, are my fortress,
     the God who shows me steadfast love.

MAY 18
~ Psalm 60:1-5

He Will Tread Down *Our Foes*

To the choirmaster: according to Shushan Eduth. A Miktam of David; for instruction; when he strove with Aram-naharaim and with Aram-zobah, and when Joab on his return struck down twelve thousand of Edom in the Valley of Salt.

1   O God, you have rejected us, broken our defenses;
       you have been angry; oh, restore us.
2   You have made the land to quake; you have torn it open;
       repair its breaches, for it totters.
3   You have made your people see hard things;
       you have given us wine to drink that made us stagger.

4   You have set up a banner for those who fear you,
       that they may flee to it from the bow.   *Selah*
5   That your beloved ones may be delivered,
       give salvation by your right hand and answer us!

Reflection

MAY 19
~ Psalm 60:6-12

6   God has spoken in his holiness:
  "With exultation I will divide up Shechem
  and portion out the Vale of Succoth.

7   Gilead is mine; Manasseh is mine;
  Ephraim is my helmet;
  Judah is my scepter.

8   Moab is my washbasin;
  upon Edom I cast my shoe;
  over Philistia I shout in triumph."

9   Who will bring me to the fortified city?
  Who will lead me to Edom?

10   Have you not rejected us, O God?
  You do not go forth, O God, with our armies.

11   Oh, grant us help against the foe,
  for vain is the salvation of man!

12   With God we shall do valiantly;
  it is he who will tread down our foes.

Reflection

MAY 20
~ Psalm 61

Lead Me to the Rock

To the choirmaster: with stringed instruments. Of David.

1 Hear my cry, O God,
   listen to my prayer;
2 from the end of the earth I call to you
   when my heart is faint.
Lead me to the rock
   that is higher than I,
3 for you have been my refuge,
   a strong tower against the enemy.

4 Let me dwell in your tent forever!
   Let me take refuge under the shelter of your wings! *Selah*
5 For you, O God, have heard my vows;
   you have given me the heritage of those who fear
      your name.

6 Prolong the life of the king;
   may his years endure to all generations!
7 May he be enthroned forever before God;
   appoint steadfast love and faithfulness to watch over him!

8 So will I ever sing praises to your name,
   as I perform my vows day after day.

Reflection

_____
_____
_____
_____

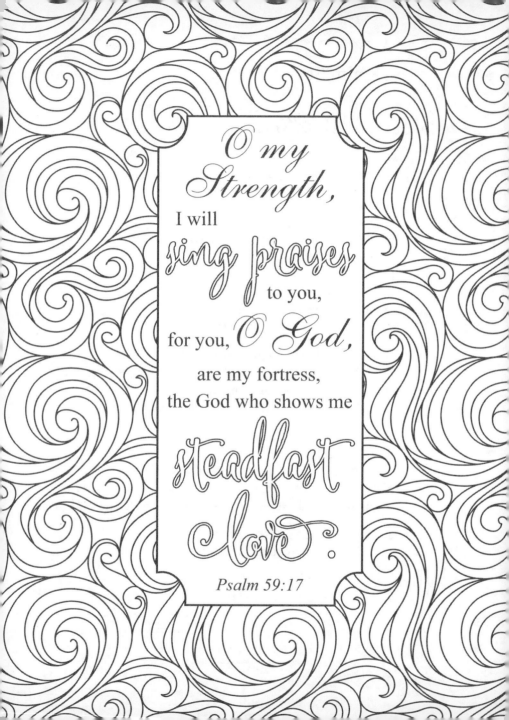

O my
Strength,
I will
sing praises
to you,
for you, O God,
are my fortress,
the God who shows me
steadfast
love.

Psalm 59:17

MAY 21
~ Psalm 62:1-6

My Soul Waits for God Alone

To the choirmaster: according to Jeduthun. A Psalm of David.

1 For God alone my soul waits in silence;
    from him comes my salvation.
2 He alone is my rock and my salvation,
    my fortress; I shall not be greatly shaken.

3 How long will all of you attack a man
    to batter him,
    like a leaning wall, a tottering fence?
4 They only plan to thrust him down from his high position.
    They take pleasure in falsehood.
They bless with their mouths,
    but inwardly they curse. *Selah*

5 For God alone, O my soul, wait in silence,
    for my hope is from him.
6 He only is my rock and my salvation,
    my fortress; I shall not be shaken.

Reflection

MAY 22
~ Psalm 62:7-12

7   On God rests my salvation and my glory;
      my mighty rock, my refuge is God.

8   Trust in him at all times, O people;
      pour out your heart before him;
      God is a refuge for us.   *Selah*

9   Those of low estate are but a breath;
      those of high estate are a delusion;
   in the balances they go up;
      they are together lighter than a breath.

10   Put no trust in extortion;
      set no vain hopes on robbery;
      if riches increase, set not your heart on them.

11   Once God has spoken;
      twice have I heard this:
   that power belongs to God,
12   and that to you, O Lord, belongs steadfast love.
   For you will render to a man
      according to his work.

Reflection

MAY 23
~ Psalm 63:1-4

My Soul Thirsts for You

A Psalm of David, when he was in the wilderness of Judah.

1   O God, you are my God; earnestly I seek you;
     my soul thirsts for you;
   my flesh faints for you,
     as in a dry and weary land where there is no water.
2   So I have looked upon you in the sanctuary,
     beholding your power and glory.
3   Because your steadfast love is better than life,
     my lips will praise you.
4   So I will bless you as long as I live;
     in your name I will lift up my hands.

Reflection

MAY 24
~ Psalm 63:5-11

5   My soul will be satisfied as with fat and rich food,
        and my mouth will praise you with joyful lips,
6   when I remember you upon my bed,
        and meditate on you in the watches of the night;
7   for you have been my help,
        and in the shadow of your wings I will sing for joy.
8   My soul clings to you;
        your right hand upholds me.

9   But those who seek to destroy my life
        shall go down into the depths of the earth;
10 they shall be given over to the power of the sword;
        they shall be a portion for jackals.
11 But the king shall rejoice in God;
        all who swear by him shall exult,
        for the mouths of liars will be stopped.

Reflection

MAY 25
~ Psalm 64:1-6

Hide Me from the Wicked

To the choirmaster. A Psalm of David.

1 Hear my voice, O God, in my complaint;
    preserve my life from dread of the enemy.
2 Hide me from the secret plots of the wicked,
    from the throng of evildoers,
3 who whet their tongues like swords,
    who aim bitter words like arrows,
4 shooting from ambush at the blameless,
    shooting at him suddenly and without fear.
5 They hold fast to their evil purpose;
    they talk of laying snares secretly,
thinking, "Who can see them?"
6   They search out injustice,
saying, "We have accomplished a diligent search."
    For the inward mind and heart of a man are deep.

Reflection

MAY 26
~ Psalm 64:7-10

7   But God shoots his arrow at them;
        they are wounded suddenly.

8   They are brought to ruin, with their own tongues turned
        against them;
        all who see them will wag their heads.

9   Then all mankind fears;
        they tell what God has brought about
        and ponder what he has done.

10   Let the righteous one rejoice in the LORD
        and take refuge in him!
        Let all the upright in heart exult!

Reflection

MAY 27
~ Psalm 65:1-8

O God of Our *Salvation*

To the choirmaster. A Psalm of David. A Song.

1   Praise is due to you, O God, in Zion,
        and to you shall vows be performed.
2   O you who hear prayer,
        to you shall all flesh come.
3   When iniquities prevail against me,
        you atone for our transgressions.
4   Blessed is the one you choose and bring near,
        to dwell in your courts!
        We shall be satisfied with the goodness of your house,
        the holiness of your temple!

5   By awesome deeds you answer us with righteousness,
        O God of our salvation,
        the hope of all the ends of the earth
        and of the farthest seas;
6   the one who by his strength established the mountains,
        being girded with might;
7   who stills the roaring of the seas,
        the roaring of their waves,
        the tumult of the peoples,
8   so that those who dwell at the ends of the earth are in awe at
        your signs.
        You make the going out of the morning and the evening to
        shout for joy.

Reflection

Because your
steadfast love
is better than life, my lips will

praise you.

So I will
bless you
as long as I live;
in your name I will lift up

my hands.

Psalm 63:3-4

MAY 28
~ Psalm 65:9-13

9   You visit the earth and water it;
        you greatly enrich it;
    the river of God is full of water;
        you provide their grain,
        for so you have prepared it.
10 You water its furrows abundantly,
        settling its ridges,
    softening it with showers,
        and blessing its growth.
11 You crown the year with your bounty;
        your wagon tracks overflow with abundance.
12 The pastures of the wilderness overflow,
        the hills gird themselves with joy,
13 the meadows clothe themselves with flocks,
        the valleys deck themselves with grain,
        they shout and sing together for joy.

Reflection

MAY 29
~ Psalm 66:1-7

How Awesome Are Your Deeds

To the choirmaster. A Song. A Psalm.

1 Shout for joy to God, all the earth;
2   sing the glory of his name;
   give to him glorious praise!
3 Say to God, "How awesome are your deeds!
   So great is your power that your enemies come cringing
      to you.
4 All the earth worships you
   and sings praises to you;
   they sing praises to your name."   *Selah*

5 Come and see what God has done:
   he is awesome in his deeds toward the children of man.
6 He turned the sea into dry land;
   they passed through the river on foot.
   There did we rejoice in him,
7   who rules by his might forever,
   whose eyes keep watch on the nations—
   let not the rebellious exalt themselves.   *Selah*

Reflection

MAY 30
~ Psalm 66:8-15

8   Bless our God, O peoples;
        let the sound of his praise be heard,
9   who has kept our soul among the living
        and has not let our feet slip.
10   For you, O God, have tested us;
        you have tried us as silver is tried.
11   You brought us into the net;
        you laid a crushing burden on our backs;
12   you let men ride over our heads;
        we went through fire and through water;
     yet you have brought us out to a place of abundance.

13   I will come into your house with burnt offerings;
        I will perform my vows to you,
14   that which my lips uttered
        and my mouth promised when I was in trouble.
15   I will offer to you burnt offerings of fattened animals,
        with the smoke of the sacrifice of rams;
     I will make an offering of bulls and goats.   *Selah*

Reflection

MAY 31
~ Psalm 66:16-20

16   Come and hear, all you who fear God,
        and I will tell what he has done for my soul.

17   I cried to him with my mouth,
        and high praise was on my tongue.

18   If I had cherished iniquity in my heart,
        the Lord would not have listened.

19   But truly God has listened;
        he has attended to the voice of my prayer.

20   Blessed be God,
        because he has not rejected my prayer
        or removed his steadfast love from me!

Reflection

JUNE 1
~ Psalm 67

Make Your Face Shine upon Us

To the choirmaster: with stringed instruments. A Psalm. A Song.

1 May God be gracious to us and bless us
 and make his face to shine upon us,   *Selah*
2 that your way may be known on earth,
 your saving power among all nations.
3 Let the peoples praise you, O God;
 let all the peoples praise you!

4 Let the nations be glad and sing for joy,
 for you judge the peoples with equity
 and guide the nations upon earth.   *Selah*
5 Let the peoples praise you, O God;
 let all the peoples praise you!

6 The earth has yielded its increase;
 God, our God, shall bless us.
7 God shall bless us;
 let all the ends of the earth fear him!

Reflection

JUNE 2
~ Psalm 68:1-6

 God Shall Scatter His Enemies

To the choirmaster. A Psalm of David. A Song.

1 God shall arise, his enemies shall be scattered;
   and those who hate him shall flee before him!
2 As smoke is driven away, so you shall drive them away;
   as wax melts before fire,
   so the wicked shall perish before God!
3 But the righteous shall be glad;
   they shall exult before God;
   they shall be jubilant with joy!

4 Sing to God, sing praises to his name;
   lift up a song to him who rides through the deserts;
   his name is the LORD;
   exult before him!
5 Father of the fatherless and protector of widows
   is God in his holy habitation.
6 God settles the solitary in a home;
   he leads out the prisoners to prosperity,
   but the rebellious dwell in a parched land.

Reflection

JUNE 3
~ Psalm 68:7-13

7 O God, when you went out before your people,
    when you marched through the wilderness,   *Selah*
8 the earth quaked, the heavens poured down rain,
    before God, the One of Sinai,
    before God, the God of Israel.
9 Rain in abundance, O God, you shed abroad;
    you restored your inheritance as it languished;
10 your flock found a dwelling in it;
    in your goodness, O God, you provided for the needy.

11 The Lord gives the word;
    the women who announce the news are a great host:
12 "The kings of the armies—they flee, they flee!"
    The women at home divide the spoil—
13   though you men lie among the sheepfolds—
    the wings of a dove covered with silver,
    its pinions with shimmering gold.

Reflection

Shout for

joy

to God, all the earth;
sing the glory
of his name;
give to him

glorious

praise !

Psalm 66:1-2

JUNE 4
~ Psalm 68:14-18

14   When the Almighty scatters kings there,
        let snow fall on Zalmon.

15   O mountain of God, mountain of Bashan;
        O many-peaked mountain, mountain of Bashan!
16   Why do you look with hatred, O many-peaked mountain,
        at the mount that God desired for his abode,
        yes, where the LORD will dwell forever?
17   The chariots of God are twice ten thousand,
        thousands upon thousands;
        the Lord is among them; Sinai is now in the sanctuary.
18   You ascended on high,
        leading a host of captives in your train
        and receiving gifts among men,
    even among the rebellious, that the LORD God may
        dwell there.

Reflection

JUNE 5
~ Psalm 68:19-23

19   Blessed be the Lord,
         who daily bears us up;
         God is our salvation.   *Selah*

20   Our God is a God of salvation,
         and to GOD, the Lord, belong deliverances from death.

21   But God will strike the heads of his enemies,
         the hairy crown of him who walks in his guilty ways.

22   The Lord said,
         " I will bring them back from Bashan,
     I will bring them back from the depths of the sea,

23   that you may strike your feet in their blood,
         that the tongues of your dogs may have their portion from
         the foe."

Reflection

JUNE 6
~ Psalm 68:24-30

24   Your procession is seen, O God,
        the procession of my God, my King, into the sanctuary—
25   the singers in front, the musicians last,
        between them virgins playing tambourines:
26   " Bless God in the great congregation,
        the LORD, O you who are of Israel's fountain!"
27   There is Benjamin, the least of them, in the lead,
        the princes of Judah in their throng,
        the princes of Zebulun, the princes of Naphtali.

28   Summon your power, O God,
        the power, O God, by which you have worked for us.
29   Because of your temple at Jerusalem
        kings shall bear gifts to you.
30   Rebuke the beasts that dwell among the reeds,
        the herd of bulls with the calves of the peoples.
    Trample underfoot those who lust after tribute;
        scatter the peoples who delight in war.

Reflection

JUNE 7
~ Psalm 68:31-35

31   Nobles shall come from Egypt;
        Cush shall hasten to stretch out her hands to God.

32   O kingdoms of the earth, sing to God;
        sing praises to the Lord,   *Selah*
33   to him who rides in the heavens, the ancient heavens;
        behold, he sends out his voice, his mighty voice.
34   Ascribe power to God,
        whose majesty is over Israel,
        and whose power is in the skies.
35   Awesome is God from his sanctuary;
        the God of Israel—he is the one who gives power and
            strength to his people.
    Blessed be God!

Reflection

JUNE 8
~ Psalm 69:1-6

Save Me, O God

To the choirmaster: according to Lilies. Of David.

1 Save me, O God!
   For the waters have come up to my neck.
2 I sink in deep mire,
   where there is no foothold;
 I have come into deep waters,
   and the flood sweeps over me.
3 I am weary with my crying out;
   my throat is parched.
 My eyes grow dim
   with waiting for my God.

4 More in number than the hairs of my head
   are those who hate me without cause;
 mighty are those who would destroy me,
   those who attack me with lies.
 What I did not steal
   must I now restore?
5 O God, you know my folly;
   the wrongs I have done are not hidden from you.

6 Let not those who hope in you be put to shame through me,
   O Lord GOD of hosts;
 let not those who seek you be brought to dishonor through me,
   O God of Israel.

Reflection

JUNE 9
~ Psalm 69:7-12

7   For it is for your sake that I have borne reproach,
       that dishonor has covered my face.

8   I have become a stranger to my brothers,
       an alien to my mother's sons.

9   For zeal for your house has consumed me,
       and the reproaches of those who reproach you have fallen
         on me.

10   When I wept and humbled my soul with fasting,
       it became my reproach.

11   When I made sackcloth my clothing,
       I became a byword to them.

12   I am the talk of those who sit in the gate,
       and the drunkards make songs about me.

Reflection

_____

_____

_____

_____

_____

_____

_____

_____

JUNE 10
~ Psalm 69:13-18

13   But as for me, my prayer is to you, O LORD.
      At an acceptable time, O God,
      in the abundance of your steadfast love answer me in your
        saving faithfulness.

14   Deliver me
      from sinking in the mire;
    let me be delivered from my enemies
    and from the deep waters.

15   Let not the flood sweep over me,
      or the deep swallow me up,
      or the pit close its mouth over me.

16   Answer me, O LORD, for your steadfast love is good;
      according to your abundant mercy, turn to me.

17   Hide not your face from your servant,
      for I am in distress; make haste to answer me.

18   Draw near to my soul, redeem me;
      ransom me because of my enemies!

Reflection

Blessed
be the Lord,
who daily bears us up;
God is our
salvation.

Psalm 68:19

JUNE 11
~ Psalm 69:19-24

19 You know my reproach,
    and my shame and my dishonor;
    my foes are all known to you.

20 Reproaches have broken my heart,
    so that I am in despair.
  I looked for pity, but there was none,
    and for comforters, but I found none.

21 They gave me poison for food,
    and for my thirst they gave me sour wine to drink.

22 Let their own table before them become a snare;
    and when they are at peace, let it become a trap.

23 Let their eyes be darkened, so that they cannot see,
    and make their loins tremble continually.

24 Pour out your indignation upon them,
    and let your burning anger overtake them.

Reflection

JUNE 12
~ Psalm 69:25-30

25   May their camp be a desolation;
      let no one dwell in their tents.

26   For they persecute him whom you have struck down,
      and they recount the pain of those you have wounded.

27   Add to them punishment upon punishment;
      may they have no acquittal from you.

28   Let them be blotted out of the book of the living;
      let them not be enrolled among the righteous.

29   But I am afflicted and in pain;
      let your salvation, O God, set me on high!

30   I will praise the name of God with a song;
      I will magnify him with thanksgiving.

Reflection

JUNE 13
~ Psalm 69:31-36

31   This will please the LORD more than an ox
        or a bull with horns and hoofs.

32   When the humble see it they will be glad;
        you who seek God, let your hearts revive.

33   For the LORD hears the needy
        and does not despise his own people who are prisoners.

34   Let heaven and earth praise him,
        the seas and everything that moves in them.

35   For God will save Zion
        and build up the cities of Judah,
    and people shall dwell there and possess it;

36   the offspring of his servants shall inherit it,
        and those who love his name shall dwell in it.

Reflection

JUNE 14
~ Psalm 70

O Lord, Do Not Delay

To the choirmaster. Of David, for the memorial offering.

1   Make haste, O God, to deliver me!
     O LORD, make haste to help me!
2   Let them be put to shame and confusion
     who seek my life!
   Let them be turned back and brought to dishonor
     who delight in my hurt!
3   Let them turn back because of their shame
     who say, "Aha, Aha!"

4   May all who seek you
     rejoice and be glad in you!
   May those who love your salvation
     say evermore, "God is great!"
5   But I am poor and needy;
     hasten to me, O God!
   You are my help and my deliverer;
     O LORD, do not delay!

Reflection

JUNE 15
~ Psalm 71:1-6

Forsake Me Not *When My Strength* Is Spent

1 In you, O Lord, do I take refuge;
  let me never be put to shame!
2 In your righteousness deliver me and rescue me;
  incline your ear to me, and save me!
3 Be to me a rock of refuge,
  to which I may continually come;
  you have given the command to save me,
  for you are my rock and my fortress.

4 Rescue me, O my God, from the hand of the wicked,
  from the grasp of the unjust and cruel man.
5 For you, O Lord, are my hope,
  my trust, O Lord, from my youth.
6 Upon you I have leaned from before my birth;
  you are he who took me from my mother's womb.
  My praise is continually of you.

Reflection

JUNE 16
~ Psalm 71:7-12

7   I have been as a portent to many,
        but you are my strong refuge.

8   My mouth is filled with your praise,
        and with your glory all the day.

9   Do not cast me off in the time of old age;
        forsake me not when my strength is spent.

10   For my enemies speak concerning me;
        those who watch for my life consult together

11   and say, "God has forsaken him;
        pursue and seize him,
        for there is none to deliver him."

12   O God, be not far from me;
        O my God, make haste to help me!

Reflection

JUNE 17
~ Psalm 71:13-18

13   May my accusers be put to shame and consumed;
    with scorn and disgrace may they be covered
    who seek my hurt.

14   But I will hope continually
    and will praise you yet more and more.

15   My mouth will tell of your righteous acts,
    of your deeds of salvation all the day,
    for their number is past my knowledge.

16   With the mighty deeds of the Lord GOD I will come;
    I will remind them of your righteousness, yours alone.

17   O God, from my youth you have taught me,
    and I still proclaim your wondrous deeds.

18   So even to old age and gray hairs,
    O God, do not forsake me,
    until I proclaim your might to another generation,
    your power to all those to come.

Reflection

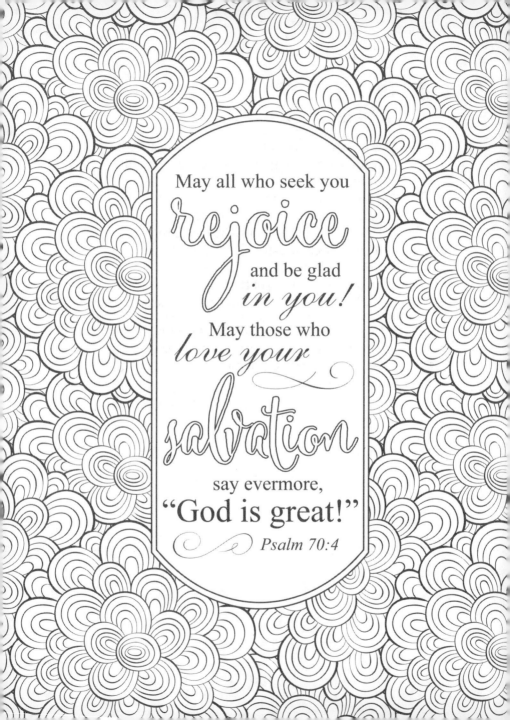

May all who seek you

rejoice

and be glad
in you!
May those who
love your

salvation

say evermore,
"God is great!"
Psalm 70:4

JUNE 18
~ Psalm 71:19-24

19   Your righteousness, O God,
       reaches the high heavens.
    You who have done great things,
       O God, who is like you?

20   You who have made me see many troubles and calamities
       will revive me again;
    from the depths of the earth
       you will bring me up again.

21   You will increase my greatness
       and comfort me again.

22   I will also praise you with the harp
       for your faithfulness, O my God;
    I will sing praises to you with the lyre,
       O Holy One of Israel.

23   My lips will shout for joy,
       when I sing praises to you;
       my soul also, which you have redeemed.

24   And my tongue will talk of your righteous help all the day long,
       for they have been put to shame and disappointed
       who sought to do me hurt.

Reflection

JUNE 19
~ Psalm 72:1-7

Give the King Your Justice

Of Solomon.

1 Give the king your justice, O God,
   and your righteousness to the royal son!
2 May he judge your people with righteousness,
   and your poor with justice!
3 Let the mountains bear prosperity for the people,
   and the hills, in righteousness!
4 May he defend the cause of the poor of the people,
   give deliverance to the children of the needy,
   and crush the oppressor!

5 May they fear you while the sun endures,
   and as long as the moon, throughout all generations!
6 May he be like rain that falls on the mown grass,
   like showers that water the earth!
7 In his days may the righteous flourish,
   and peace abound, till the moon be no more!

Reflection

JUNE 20
~ Psalm 72:8-14

8   May he have dominion from sea to sea,
        and from the River to the ends of the earth!

9   May desert tribes bow down before him,
        and his enemies lick the dust!

10   May the kings of Tarshish and of the coastlands
        render him tribute;
    may the kings of Sheba and Seba
        bring gifts!

11   May all kings fall down before him,
        all nations serve him!

12   For he delivers the needy when he calls,
        the poor and him who has no helper.

13   He has pity on the weak and the needy,
        and saves the lives of the needy.

14   From oppression and violence he redeems their life,
        and precious is their blood in his sight.

Reflection

JUNE 21
~ Psalm 72:15-20

15 Long may he live;
    may gold of Sheba be given to him!
    May prayer be made for him continually,
    and blessings invoked for him all the day!
16 May there be abundance of grain in the land;
    on the tops of the mountains may it wave;
    may its fruit be like Lebanon;
    and may people blossom in the cities
    like the grass of the field!
17 May his name endure forever,
    his fame continue as long as the sun!
    May people be blessed in him,
    all nations call him blessed!

18 Blessed be the Lord, the God of Israel,
    who alone does wondrous things.
19 Blessed be his glorious name forever;
    may the whole earth be filled with his glory!
    Amen and Amen!

20 The prayers of David, the son of Jesse, are ended.

Reflection

JUNE 22
~ Psalm 73:1-7

 God Is My *Strength* and Portion *Forever*

A Psalm of Asaph.

1 Truly God is good to Israel,
   to those who are pure in heart.
2 But as for me, my feet had almost stumbled,
   my steps had nearly slipped.
3 For I was envious of the arrogant
   when I saw the prosperity of the wicked.

4 For they have no pangs until death;
   their bodies are fat and sleek.
5 They are not in trouble as others are;
   they are not stricken like the rest of mankind.
6 Therefore pride is their necklace;
   violence covers them as a garment.
7 Their eyes swell out through fatness;
   their hearts overflow with follies.

Reflection

JUNE 23
~ Psalm 73:8-15

8   They scoff and speak with malice;
     loftily they threaten oppression.
9   They set their mouths against the heavens,
     and their tongue struts through the earth.
10   Therefore his people turn back to them,
     and find no fault in them.
11   And they say, "How can God know?
     Is there knowledge in the Most High?"
12   Behold, these are the wicked;
     always at ease, they increase in riches.
13   All in vain have I kept my heart clean
     and washed my hands in innocence.
14   For all the day long I have been stricken
     and rebuked every morning.
15   If I had said, "I will speak thus,"
     I would have betrayed the generation of your children.

Reflection

JUNE 24
~ Psalm 73:16-20

16   But when I thought how to understand this,
          it seemed to me a wearisome task,
17   until I went into the sanctuary of God;
          then I discerned their end.

18   Truly you set them in slippery places;
          you make them fall to ruin.
19   How they are destroyed in a moment,
          swept away utterly by terrors!
20   Like a dream when one awakes,
          O Lord, when you rouse yourself, you despise them as
          phantoms.

Reflection

My lips will shout *for joy,* when I *sing praises to you;* my soul also, which you have *redeemed.*

Psalm 71:23

JUNE 25
~ Psalm 73:21-28

21   When my soul was embittered,
        when I was pricked in heart,
22   I was brutish and ignorant;
        I was like a beast toward you.

23   Nevertheless, I am continually with you;
        you hold my right hand.
24   You guide me with your counsel,
        and afterward you will receive me to glory.
25   Whom have I in heaven but you?
        And there is nothing on earth that I desire besides you.
26   My flesh and my heart may fail,
        but God is the strength of my heart and my
            portion forever.

27   For behold, those who are far from you shall perish;
        you put an end to everyone who is unfaithful to you.
28   But for me it is good to be near God;
        I have made the Lord GOD my refuge,
        that I may tell of all your works.

Reflection

JUNE 26
~ Psalm 74:1-6

Arise, O God, Defend Your Cause

A Maskil of Asaph.

1 O God, why do you cast us off forever?
   Why does your anger smoke against the sheep
      of your pasture?
2 Remember your congregation, which you have
      purchased of old,
   which you have redeemed to be the tribe of your heritage!
   Remember Mount Zion, where you have dwelt.
3 Direct your steps to the perpetual ruins;
   the enemy has destroyed everything in the sanctuary!

4 Your foes have roared in the midst of your meeting place;
   they set up their own signs for signs.
5 They were like those who swing axes
   in a forest of trees.
6 And all its carved wood
   they broke down with hatchets and hammers.

Reflection

JUNE 27
~ Psalm 74:7-11

7   They set your sanctuary on fire;
        they profaned the dwelling place of your name,
        bringing it down to the ground.

8   They said to themselves, "We will utterly subdue them";
        they burned all the meeting places of God in the land.

9   We do not see our signs;
        there is no longer any prophet,
        and there is none among us who knows how long.

10   How long, O God, is the foe to scoff?
        Is the enemy to revile your name forever?

11   Why do you hold back your hand, your right hand?
        Take it from the fold of your garment and destroy them!

Reflection

JUNE 28
~ Psalm 74:12-17

12   Yet God my King is from of old,
         working salvation in the midst of the earth.
13   You divided the sea by your might;
         you broke the heads of the sea monsters on the waters.
14   You crushed the heads of Leviathan;
         you gave him as food for the creatures of the wilderness.
15   You split open springs and brooks;
         you dried up ever-flowing streams.
16   Yours is the day, yours also the night;
         you have established the heavenly lights and the sun.
17   You have fixed all the boundaries of the earth;
         you have made summer and winter.

Reflection

JUNE 29
~ Psalm 74:18-23

18   Remember this, O LORD, how the enemy scoffs,
        and a foolish people reviles your name.
19   Do not deliver the soul of your dove to the wild beasts;
        do not forget the life of your poor forever.

20   Have regard for the covenant,
        for the dark places of the land are full of the habitations of
            violence.
21   Let not the downtrodden turn back in shame;
        let the poor and needy praise your name.

22   Arise, O God, defend your cause;
        remember how the foolish scoff at you all the day!
23   Do not forget the clamor of your foes,
        the uproar of those who rise against you,
            which goes up continually!

Reflection

JUNE 30
~ Psalm 75:1-5

God Will Judge with Equity

To the choirmaster: according to Do Not Destroy. A Psalm of Asaph. A Song.

1 We give thanks to you, O God;
we give thanks, for your name is near.
We recount your wondrous deeds.

2 " At the set time that I appoint
I will judge with equity.

3 When the earth totters, and all its inhabitants,
it is I who keep steady its pillars.   *Selah*

4 I say to the boastful, 'Do not boast,'
and to the wicked, 'Do not lift up your horn;

5 do not lift up your horn on high,
or speak with haughty neck.'"

Reflection

JULY 1
~ Psalm 75:6-10

6   For not from the east or from the west
       and not from the wilderness comes lifting up,
7   but it is God who executes judgment,
       putting down one and lifting up another.
8   For in the hand of the LORD there is a cup
       with foaming wine, well mixed,
and he pours out from it,
       and all the wicked of the earth
       shall drain it down to the dregs.

9   But I will declare it forever;
       I will sing praises to the God of Jacob.
10   All the horns of the wicked I will cut off,
       but the horns of the righteous shall be lifted up.

Reflection

JULY 2
~ Psalm 76:1-6

 Can Stand Before You?

To the choirmaster: with stringed instruments. A Psalm of Asaph. A Song.

1 In Judah God is known;
    his name is great in Israel.
2 His abode has been established in Salem,
    his dwelling place in Zion.
3 There he broke the flashing arrows,
    the shield, the sword, and the weapons of war.   *Selah*

4 Glorious are you, more majestic
    than the mountains full of prey.
5 The stouthearted were stripped of their spoil;
    they sank into sleep;
all the men of war
    were unable to use their hands.
6 At your rebuke, O God of Jacob,
    both rider and horse lay stunned.

Reflection

We give
thanks
to you, O God;
we give thanks,
for your name is near.
We recount your
wondrous
deeds.
Psalm 75:1

JULY 3
~ Psalm 76:7-12

7   But you, you are to be feared!
        Who can stand before you
        when once your anger is roused?

8   From the heavens you uttered judgment;
        the earth feared and was still,

9   when God arose to establish judgment,
        to save all the humble of the earth.   *Selah*

10   Surely the wrath of man shall praise you;
        the remnant of wrath you will put on like a belt.

11   Make your vows to the Lord your God and perform them;
        let all around him bring gifts
        to him who is to be feared,

12   who cuts off the spirit of princes,
        who is to be feared by the kings of the earth.

Reflection

JULY 4
~ Psalm 77:1-6a

In the Day of Trouble I Seek the Lord

To the choirmaster: according to Jeduthun. A Psalm of Asaph.

1   I cry aloud to God,
        aloud to God, and he will hear me.

2   In the day of my trouble I seek the Lord;
        in the night my hand is stretched out without wearying;
        my soul refuses to be comforted.

3   When I remember God, I moan;
        when I meditate, my spirit faints.   *Selah*

4   You hold my eyelids open;
        I am so troubled that I cannot speak.

5   I consider the days of old,
        the years long ago.

6   I said, "Let me remember my song in the night;
        let me meditate in my heart."

Reflection

JULY 5
~ Psalm 77:6b-12

Then my spirit made a diligent search:

7   "Will the Lord spurn forever,
      and never again be favorable?

8   Has his steadfast love forever ceased?
      Are his promises at an end for all time?

9   Has God forgotten to be gracious?
      Has he in anger shut up his compassion?"   *Selah*

10   Then I said, "I will appeal to this,
      to the years of the right hand of the Most High."

11   I will remember the deeds of the LORD;
      yes, I will remember your wonders of old.

12   I will ponder all your work,
      and meditate on your mighty deeds.

Reflection

JULY 6
~ Psalm 77:13-20

13   Your way, O God, is holy.
        What god is great like our God?
14   You are the God who works wonders;
        you have made known your might among the peoples.
15   You with your arm redeemed your people,
        the children of Jacob and Joseph.   *Selah*

16   When the waters saw you, O God,
        when the waters saw you, they were afraid;
        indeed, the deep trembled.
17   The clouds poured out water;
        the skies gave forth thunder;
        your arrows flashed on every side.
18   The crash of your thunder was in the whirlwind;
        your lightnings lighted up the world;
        the earth trembled and shook.
19   Your way was through the sea,
        your path through the great waters;
        yet your footprints were unseen.
20   You led your people like a flock
        by the hand of Moses and Aaron.

Reflection

JULY 7
~ Psalm 78:1-8

Tell the Coming Generation

A Maskil of Asaph.

1 Give ear, O my people, to my teaching;
   incline your ears to the words of my mouth!
2 I will open my mouth in a parable;
   I will utter dark sayings from of old,
3 things that we have heard and known,
   that our fathers have told us.
4 We will not hide them from their children,
      but tell to the coming generation
   the glorious deeds of the LORD, and his might,
   and the wonders that he has done.

5 He established a testimony in Jacob
      and appointed a law in Israel,
   which he commanded our fathers
      to teach to their children,
6 that the next generation might know them,
      the children yet unborn,
   and arise and tell them to their children,
7   so that they should set their hope in God
   and not forget the works of God,
      but keep his commandments;
8 and that they should not be like their fathers,
      a stubborn and rebellious generation,
   a generation whose heart was not steadfast,
      whose spirit was not faithful to God.

Reflection

JULY 8
~ Psalm 78:9-16

9   The Ephraimites, armed with the bow,
      turned back on the day of battle.
10   They did not keep God's covenant,
      but refused to walk according to his law.
11   They forgot his works
      and the wonders that he had shown them.
12   In the sight of their fathers he performed wonders
      in the land of Egypt, in the fields of Zoan.
13   He divided the sea and let them pass through it,
      and made the waters stand like a heap.
14   In the daytime he led them with a cloud,
      and all the night with a fiery light.
15   He split rocks in the wilderness
      and gave them drink abundantly as from the deep.
16   He made streams come out of the rock
      and caused waters to flow down like rivers.

Reflection

J U L Y 9
~ Psalm 78:17-25

17   Yet they sinned still more against him,
         rebelling against the Most High in the desert.
18   They tested God in their heart
         by demanding the food they craved.
19   They spoke against God, saying,
         " Can God spread a table in the wilderness?
20   He struck the rock so that water gushed out
         and streams overflowed.
     Can he also give bread
         or provide meat for his people?"

21   Therefore, when the LORD heard, he was full of wrath;
         a fire was kindled against Jacob;
         his anger rose against Israel,
22   because they did not believe in God
         and did not trust his saving power.
23   Yet he commanded the skies above
         and opened the doors of heaven,
24   and he rained down on them manna to eat
         and gave them the grain of heaven.
25   Man ate of the bread of the angels;
         he sent them food in abundance.

Reflection

_____

_____
_____
_____

I cry
aloud to
God,
aloud
to God,
and he will
hear me.
Psalm 77:1

JULY 10
~ Psalm 78:26-34

26 He caused the east wind to blow in the heavens,
    and by his power he led out the south wind;
27 he rained meat on them like dust,
    winged birds like the sand of the seas;
28 he let them fall in the midst of their camp,
    all around their dwellings.
29 And they ate and were well filled,
    for he gave them what they craved.
30 But before they had satisfied their craving,
    while the food was still in their mouths,
31 the anger of God rose against them,
    and he killed the strongest of them
    and laid low the young men of Israel.

32 In spite of all this, they still sinned;
    despite his wonders, they did not believe.
33 So he made their days vanish like a breath,
    and their years in terror.
34 When he killed them, they sought him;
    they repented and sought God earnestly.

Reflection

JULY 11
~ Psalm 78:35-43

35   They remembered that God was their rock,
        the Most High God their redeemer.
36   But they flattered him with their mouths;
        they lied to him with their tongues.
37   Their heart was not steadfast toward him;
        they were not faithful to his covenant.
38   Yet he, being compassionate,
        atoned for their iniquity
        and did not destroy them;
    he restrained his anger often
        and did not stir up all his wrath.
39   He remembered that they were but flesh,
        a wind that passes and comes not again.
40   How often they rebelled against him in the wilderness
        and grieved him in the desert!
41   They tested God again and again
        and provoked the Holy One of Israel.
42   They did not remember his power
        or the day when he redeemed them from the foe,
43   when he performed his signs in Egypt
        and his marvels in the fields of Zoan.

Reflection

JULY 12
~ Psalm 78:44-52

44   He turned their rivers to blood,
       so that they could not drink of their streams.

45   He sent among them swarms of flies, which devoured them,
       and frogs, which destroyed them.

46   He gave their crops to the destroying locust
       and the fruit of their labor to the locust.

47   He destroyed their vines with hail
       and their sycamores with frost.

48   He gave over their cattle to the hail
       and their flocks to thunderbolts.

49   He let loose on them his burning anger,
       wrath, indignation, and distress,
       a company of destroying angels.

50   He made a path for his anger;
       he did not spare them from death,
       but gave their lives over to the plague.

51   He struck down every firstborn in Egypt,
       the firstfruits of their strength in the tents of Ham.

52   Then he led out his people like sheep
       and guided them in the wilderness like a flock.

Reflection

JULY 13
~ Psalm 78:53-61

53   He led them in safety, so that they were not afraid,
      but the sea overwhelmed their enemies.
54   And he brought them to his holy land,
      to the mountain which his right hand had won.
55   He drove out nations before them;
      he apportioned them for a possession
      and settled the tribes of Israel in their tents.

56   Yet they tested and rebelled against the Most High God
      and did not keep his testimonies,
57   but turned away and acted treacherously like their fathers;
      they twisted like a deceitful bow.
58   For they provoked him to anger with their high places;
      they moved him to jealousy with their idols.
59   When God heard, he was full of wrath,
      and he utterly rejected Israel.
60   He forsook his dwelling at Shiloh,
      the tent where he dwelt among mankind,
61   and delivered his power to captivity,
      his glory to the hand of the foe.

Reflection

JULY 14
~ Psalm 78:62-72

62 He gave his people over to the sword
   and vented his wrath on his heritage.
63 Fire devoured their young men,
   and their young women had no marriage song.
64 Their priests fell by the sword,
   and their widows made no lamentation.
65 Then the Lord awoke as from sleep,
   like a strong man shouting because of wine.
66 And he put his adversaries to rout;
   he put them to everlasting shame.

67 He rejected the tent of Joseph;
   he did not choose the tribe of Ephraim,
68 but he chose the tribe of Judah,
   Mount Zion, which he loves.
69 He built his sanctuary like the high heavens,
   like the earth, which he has founded forever.
70 He chose David his servant
   and took him from the sheepfolds;
71 from following the nursing ewes he brought him
   to shepherd Jacob his people,
   Israel his inheritance.
72 With upright heart he shepherded them
   and guided them with his skillful hand.

Reflection

JULY 15
~ Psalm 79:1-7

How Long, O Lord?

A Psalm of Asaph.

1   O God, the nations have come into your inheritance;
     they have defiled your holy temple;
     they have laid Jerusalem in ruins.

2   They have given the bodies of your servants
     to the birds of the heavens for food,
     the flesh of your faithful to the beasts of the earth.

3   They have poured out their blood like water
     all around Jerusalem,
     and there was no one to bury them.

4   We have become a taunt to our neighbors,
     mocked and derided by those around us.

5   How long, O LORD? Will you be angry forever?
     Will your jealousy burn like fire?

6   Pour out your anger on the nations
     that do not know you,
   and on the kingdoms
     that do not call upon your name!

7   For they have devoured Jacob
     and laid waste his habitation.

Reflection

JULY 16
~ Psalm 79:8-13

8   Do not remember against us our former iniquities;
        let your compassion come speedily to meet us,
        for we are brought very low.
9   Help us, O God of our salvation,
        for the glory of your name;
    deliver us, and atone for our sins,
        for your name's sake!
10   Why should the nations say,
        "Where is their God?"
    Let the avenging of the outpoured blood of your servants
        be known among the nations before our eyes!

11   Let the groans of the prisoners come before you;
        according to your great power, preserve those
            doomed to die!
12   Return sevenfold into the lap of our neighbors
        the taunts with which they have taunted you, O Lord!
13   But we your people, the sheep of your pasture,
        will give thanks to you forever;
        from generation to generation we will recount
            your praise.

Reflection

But we your people, *the sheep* of your *pasture,* will give *thanks to you forever;* from generation to generation we will recount your *praise.*

Psalm 79:13

JULY 17
~ Psalm 80:1-7

Restore Us, O God

To the choirmaster: according to Lilies. A Testimony. Of Asaph, a Psalm.

1 Give ear, O Shepherd of Israel,
   you who lead Joseph like a flock.
You who are enthroned upon the cherubim, shine forth.
2   Before Ephraim and Benjamin and Manasseh,
stir up your might
   and come to save us!

3 Restore us, O God;
   let your face shine, that we may be saved!

4 O LORD God of hosts,
   how long will you be angry with your people's prayers?
5 You have fed them with the bread of tears
   and given them tears to drink in full measure.
6 You make us an object of contention for our neighbors,
   and our enemies laugh among themselves.

7 Restore us, O God of hosts;
   let your face shine, that we may be saved!

Reflection

JULY 18
~ Psalm 80:8-13

8   You brought a vine out of Egypt;
    you drove out the nations and planted it.
9   You cleared the ground for it;
    it took deep root and filled the land.
10   The mountains were covered with its shade,
    the mighty cedars with its branches.
11   It sent out its branches to the sea
    and its shoots to the River.
12   Why then have you broken down its walls,
    so that all who pass along the way pluck its fruit?
13   The boar from the forest ravages it,
    and all that move in the field feed on it.

Reflection

JULY 19
~ Psalm 80:14-19

14   Turn again, O God of hosts!
     Look down from heaven, and see;
   have regard for this vine,

15   the stock that your right hand planted,
     and for the son whom you made strong for yourself.

16   They have burned it with fire; they have cut it down;
     may they perish at the rebuke of your face!

17   But let your hand be on the man of your right hand,
     the son of man whom you have made strong for yourself!

18   Then we shall not turn back from you;
     give us life, and we will call upon your name!

19   Restore us, O Lord God of hosts!
     Let your face shine, that we may be saved!

Reflection

JULY 20
~ Psalm 81:1-8

Oh, That My People Would _Listen to Me_

To the choirmaster: according to The Gittith. Of Asaph.

1 Sing aloud to God our strength;
   shout for joy to the God of Jacob!
2 Raise a song; sound the tambourine,
   the sweet lyre with the harp.
3 Blow the trumpet at the new moon,
   at the full moon, on our feast day.

4 For it is a statute for Israel,
   a rule of the God of Jacob.
5 He made it a decree in Joseph
   when he went out over the land of Egypt.
   I hear a language I had not known:
6 " I relieved your shoulder of the burden;
   your hands were freed from the basket.
7 In distress you called, and I delivered you;
   I answered you in the secret place of thunder;
   I tested you at the waters of Meribah.   *Selah*
8 Hear, O my people, while I admonish you!
   O Israel, if you would but listen to me!

Reflection

JULY 21
~ Psalm 81:9-16

9   There shall be no strange god among you;
        you shall not bow down to a foreign god.

10   I am the LORD your God,
        who brought you up out of the land of Egypt.
        Open your mouth wide, and I will fill it.

11   " But my people did not listen to my voice;
        Israel would not submit to me.

12   So I gave them over to their stubborn hearts,
        to follow their own counsels.

13   Oh, that my people would listen to me,
        that Israel would walk in my ways!

14   I would soon subdue their enemies
        and turn my hand against their foes.

15   Those who hate the LORD would cringe toward him,
        and their fate would last forever.

16   But he would feed you with the finest of the wheat,
        and with honey from the rock I would satisfy you."

Reflection

JULY 22
~ Psalm 82

 Rescue the Weak and Needy

A Psalm of Asaph.

1 God has taken his place in the divine council;
   in the midst of the gods he holds judgment:
2 " How long will you judge unjustly
   and show partiality to the wicked?   *Selah*
3 Give justice to the weak and the fatherless;
   maintain the right of the afflicted and the destitute.
4 Rescue the weak and the needy;
   deliver them from the hand of the wicked."

5 They have neither knowledge nor understanding,
   they walk about in darkness;
   all the foundations of the earth are shaken.

6 I said, "You are gods,
   sons of the Most High, all of you;
7 nevertheless, like men you shall die,
   and fall like any prince."

8 Arise, O God, judge the earth;
   for you shall inherit all the nations!

Reflection

JULY 23
~ Psalm 83:1-8

O God, Do Not Keep Silence

A Song. A Psalm of Asaph.

1 O God, do not keep silence;
    do not hold your peace or be still, O God!
2 For behold, your enemies make an uproar;
    those who hate you have raised their heads.
3 They lay crafty plans against your people;
    they consult together against your treasured ones.
4 They say, "Come, let us wipe them out as a nation;
    let the name of Israel be remembered no more!"
5 For they conspire with one accord;
    against you they make a covenant—
6 the tents of Edom and the Ishmaelites,
    Moab and the Hagrites,
7 Gebal and Ammon and Amalek,
    Philistia with the inhabitants of Tyre;
8 Asshur also has joined them;
    they are the strong arm of the children of Lot.   *Selah*

Reflection

Arise, O God,
judge the earth;
for you shall inherit all the nations!
Psalm 82:8

JULY 24
~ Psalm 83:9-18

9   Do to them as you did to Midian,
        as to Sisera and Jabin at the river Kishon,

10   who were destroyed at En-dor,
        who became dung for the ground.

11   Make their nobles like Oreb and Zeeb,
        all their princes like Zebah and Zalmunna,

12   who said, "Let us take possession for ourselves
        of the pastures of God."

13   O my God, make them like whirling dust,
        like chaff before the wind.

14   As fire consumes the forest,
        as the flame sets the mountains ablaze,

15   so may you pursue them with your tempest
        and terrify them with your hurricane!

16   Fill their faces with shame,
        that they may seek your name, O LORD.

17   Let them be put to shame and dismayed forever;
        let them perish in disgrace,

18   that they may know that you alone,
        whose name is the LORD,
        are the Most High over all the earth.

Reflection

JULY 25
~ Psalm 84:1-6

My Soul Longs for the Courts of the Lord

To the choirmaster: according to The Gittith. A Psalm of the Sons of Korah.

1 How lovely is your dwelling place,
   O Lord of hosts!
2 My soul longs, yes, faints
   for the courts of the Lord;
   my heart and flesh sing for joy
   to the living God.

3 Even the sparrow finds a home,
   and the swallow a nest for herself,
   where she may lay her young,
   at your altars, O Lord of hosts,
   my King and my God.
4 Blessed are those who dwell in your house,
   ever singing your praise!   *Selah*

5 Blessed are those whose strength is in you,
   in whose heart are the highways to Zion.
6 As they go through the Valley of Baca
   they make it a place of springs;
   the early rain also covers it with pools.

Reflection

_____
_____
_____
_____
_____

JULY 26
~ Psalm 84:7-12

7   They go from strength to strength;
        each one appears before God in Zion.

8   O LORD God of hosts, hear my prayer;
        give ear, O God of Jacob!   *Selah*

9   Behold our shield, O God;
        look on the face of your anointed!

10   For a day in your courts is better
        than a thousand elsewhere.
    I would rather be a doorkeeper in the house of my God
        than dwell in the tents of wickedness.

11   For the LORD God is a sun and shield;
        the LORD bestows favor and honor.
    No good thing does he withhold
        from those who walk uprightly.

12   O LORD of hosts,
        blessed is the one who trusts in you!

Reflection

JULY 27
~ Psalm 85:1-7

To the choirmaster. A Psalm of the Sons of Korah.

1 LORD, you were favorable to your land;
   you restored the fortunes of Jacob.
2 You forgave the iniquity of your people;
   you covered all their sin.   *Selah*
3 You withdrew all your wrath;
   you turned from your hot anger.

4 Restore us again, O God of our salvation,
   and put away your indignation toward us!
5 Will you be angry with us forever?
   Will you prolong your anger to all generations?
6 Will you not revive us again,
   that your people may rejoice in you?
7 Show us your steadfast love, O LORD,
   and grant us your salvation.

Reflection

JULY 28
~ Psalm 85:8-13

8   Let me hear what God the LORD will speak,
        for he will speak peace to his people, to his saints;
        but let them not turn back to folly.

9   Surely his salvation is near to those who fear him,
        that glory may dwell in our land.

10   Steadfast love and faithfulness meet;
        righteousness and peace kiss each other.

11   Faithfulness springs up from the ground,
        and righteousness looks down from the sky.

12   Yes, the LORD will give what is good,
        and our land will yield its increase.

13   Righteousness will go before him
        and make his footsteps a way.

Reflection

JULY 29
~ Psalm 86:1-7

Great Is Your Steadfast Love

A Prayer of David.

1   Incline your ear, O LORD, and answer me,
     for I am poor and needy.

2   Preserve my life, for I am godly;
     save your servant, who trusts in you—you are my God.

3   Be gracious to me, O Lord,
     for to you do I cry all the day.

4   Gladden the soul of your servant,
     for to you, O Lord, do I lift up my soul.

5   For you, O Lord, are good and forgiving,
     abounding in steadfast love to all who call upon you.

6   Give ear, O LORD, to my prayer;
     listen to my plea for grace.

7   In the day of my trouble I call upon you,
     for you answer me.

Reflection

JULY 30
~ Psalm 86:8-17

8   There is none like you among the gods, O Lord,
      nor are there any works like yours.
9   All the nations you have made shall come
      and worship before you, O Lord,
      and shall glorify your name.
10 For you are great and do wondrous things;
      you alone are God.
11 Teach me your way, O LORD,
      that I may walk in your truth;
      unite my heart to fear your name.
12 I give thanks to you, O Lord my God, with my whole heart,
      and I will glorify your name forever.
13 For great is your steadfast love toward me;
      you have delivered my soul from the depths of Sheol.

14 O God, insolent men have risen up against me;
      a band of ruthless men seeks my life,
      and they do not set you before them.
15 But you, O Lord, are a God merciful and gracious,
      slow to anger and abounding in steadfast love
        and faithfulness.
16 Turn to me and be gracious to me;
      give your strength to your servant,
      and save the son of your maidservant.
17 Show me a sign of your favor,
      that those who hate me may see and be put to shame
      because you, LORD, have helped me and comforted me.

Reflection

How
lovely
is your
dwelling place,
O LORD of hosts!
My soul longs, yes, faints
for the courts of
the LORD;
my heart
and flesh sing for
joy to the
living God.

Psalm 84:1-2

JULY 31
~ Psalm 87

Glorious Things of You Are Spoken

A Psalm of the Sons of Korah. A Song.

1 On the holy mount stands the city he founded;
2   the LORD loves the gates of Zion
    more than all the dwelling places of Jacob.
3 Glorious things of you are spoken,
    O city of God.   *Selah*

4   Among those who know me I mention Rahab and Babylon;
    behold, Philistia and Tyre, with Cush—
    "This one was born there," they say.
5   And of Zion it shall be said,
    "This one and that one were born in her";
    for the Most High himself will establish her.
6   The LORD records as he registers the peoples,
    "This one was born there."   *Selah*

7   Singers and dancers alike say,
    "All my springs are in you."

Reflection

AUGUST 1
~ Psalm 88:1-7

I Cry Out *Day and Night Before You*

A Song. A Psalm of the Sons of Korah. To the choirmaster: according to Mahalath Leannoth. A Maskil of Heman the Ezrahite.

1 O LORD, God of my salvation,
   I cry out day and night before you.
2 Let my prayer come before you;
   incline your ear to my cry!

3 For my soul is full of troubles,
   and my life draws near to Sheol.
4 I am counted among those who go down to the pit;
   I am a man who has no strength,
5 like one set loose among the dead,
   like the slain that lie in the grave,
   like those whom you remember no more,
   for they are cut off from your hand.
6 You have put me in the depths of the pit,
   in the regions dark and deep.
7 Your wrath lies heavy upon me,
   and you overwhelm me with all your waves.   *Selah*

Reflection

AUGUST 2
~ Psalm 88:8-12

8   You have caused my companions to shun me;
       you have made me a horror to them.
    I am shut in so that I cannot escape;
9   my eye grows dim through sorrow.
    Every day I call upon you, O LORD;
       I spread out my hands to you.
10   Do you work wonders for the dead?
       Do the departed rise up to praise you?   *Selah*
11   Is your steadfast love declared in the grave,
       or your faithfulness in Abaddon?
12   Are your wonders known in the darkness,
       or your righteousness in the land of forgetfulness?

Reflection

AUGUST 3
~ Psalm 88:13-18

13 But I, O LORD, cry to you;
    in the morning my prayer comes before you.
14 O LORD, why do you cast my soul away?
    Why do you hide your face from me?
15 Afflicted and close to death from my youth up,
    I suffer your terrors; I am helpless.
16 Your wrath has swept over me;
    your dreadful assaults destroy me.
17 They surround me like a flood all day long;
    they close in on me together.
18 You have caused my beloved and my friend to shun me;
    my companions have become darkness.

Reflection

AUGUST 4
~ Psalm 89:1-7

I Will *Sing* of the *Steadfast Love* of the Lord

A Maskil of Ethan the Ezrahite.

1 I will sing of the steadfast love of the Lord, forever;
    with my mouth I will make known your faithfulness
        to all generations.
2 For I said, "Steadfast love will be built up forever;
    in the heavens you will establish your faithfulness."
3 You have said, "I have made a covenant with my chosen one;
    I have sworn to David my servant:
4 'I will establish your offspring forever,
    and build your throne for all generations.'" *Selah*

5 Let the heavens praise your wonders, O Lord,
    your faithfulness in the assembly of the holy ones!
6 For who in the skies can be compared to the Lord?
    Who among the heavenly beings is like the Lord,
7 a God greatly to be feared in the council of the holy ones,
    and awesome above all who are around him?

Reflection

AUGUST 5
~ Psalm 89:8-14

8   O LORD God of hosts,
      who is mighty as you are, O LORD,
      with your faithfulness all around you?
9   You rule the raging of the sea;
      when its waves rise, you still them.
10 You crushed Rahab like a carcass;
      you scattered your enemies with your mighty arm.
11 The heavens are yours; the earth also is yours;
      the world and all that is in it, you have founded them.
12 The north and the south, you have created them;
      Tabor and Hermon joyously praise your name.
13 You have a mighty arm;
      strong is your hand, high your right hand.
14 Righteousness and justice are the foundation of your throne;
      steadfast love and faithfulness go before you.

AUGUST 6
~ Psalm 89:15-22

15 Blessed are the people who know the festal shout,
    who walk, O LORD, in the light of your face,
16 who exult in your name all the day
    and in your righteousness are exalted.
17 For you are the glory of their strength;
    by your favor our horn is exalted.
18 For our shield belongs to the LORD,
    our king to the Holy One of Israel.

19 Of old you spoke in a vision to your godly one, and said:
    " I have granted help to one who is mighty;
    I have exalted one chosen from the people.
20 I have found David, my servant;
    with my holy oil I have anointed him,
21 so that my hand shall be established with him;
    my arm also shall strengthen him.
22 The enemy shall not outwit him;
    the wicked shall not humble him.

Reflection

AUGUST 7
~ Psalm 89:23-29

23   I will crush his foes before him
       and strike down those who hate him.

24   My faithfulness and my steadfast love shall be with him,
       and in my name shall his horn be exalted.

25   I will set his hand on the sea
       and his right hand on the rivers.

26   He shall cry to me, 'You are my Father,
       my God, and the Rock of my salvation.'

27   And I will make him the firstborn,
       the highest of the kings of the earth.

28   My steadfast love I will keep for him forever,
       and my covenant will stand firm for him.

29   I will establish his offspring forever
       and his throne as the days of the heavens.

Reflection

AUGUST 8
~ Psalm 89:30-37

30   If his children forsake my law
       and do not walk according to my rules,
31   if they violate my statutes
       and do not keep my commandments,
32   then I will punish their transgression with the rod
       and their iniquity with stripes,
33   but I will not remove from him my steadfast love
       or be false to my faithfulness.
34   I will not violate my covenant
       or alter the word that went forth from my lips.
35   Once for all I have sworn by my holiness;
       I will not lie to David.
36   His offspring shall endure forever,
       his throne as long as the sun before me.
37   Like the moon it shall be established forever,
       a faithful witness in the skies."   *Selah*

Reflection

AUGUST 9
~ Psalm 89:38-45

38   But now you have cast off and rejected;
        you are full of wrath against your anointed.

39   You have renounced the covenant with your servant;
        you have defiled his crown in the dust.

40   You have breached all his walls;
        you have laid his strongholds in ruins.

41   All who pass by plunder him;
        he has become the scorn of his neighbors.

42   You have exalted the right hand of his foes;
        you have made all his enemies rejoice.

43   You have also turned back the edge of his sword,
        and you have not made him stand in battle.

44   You have made his splendor to cease
        and cast his throne to the ground.

45   You have cut short the days of his youth;
        you have covered him with shame.   *Selah*

Reflection

AUGUST 10
~ Psalm 89:46-52

46   How long, O LORD? Will you hide yourself forever?
        How long will your wrath burn like fire?
47   Remember how short my time is!
        For what vanity you have created all the children of man!
48   What man can live and never see death?
        Who can deliver his soul from the power of Sheol?   *Selah*

49   Lord, where is your steadfast love of old,
        which by your faithfulness you swore to David?
50   Remember, O Lord, how your servants are mocked,
        and how I bear in my heart the insults of all the
            many nations,
51   with which your enemies mock, O LORD,
        with which they mock the footsteps of your anointed.

52   Blessed be the LORD forever!
        Amen and Amen.

Reflection

AUGUST 11
~ Psalm 90:1-8

From Everlasting to Everlasting

A Prayer of Moses, the man of God.

1 Lord, you have been our dwelling place
  in all generations.
2 Before the mountains were brought forth,
  or ever you had formed the earth and the world,
  from everlasting to everlasting you are God.

3 You return man to dust
  and say, "Return, O children of man!"
4 For a thousand years in your sight
  are but as yesterday when it is past,
  or as a watch in the night.

5 You sweep them away as with a flood; they are like a dream,
  like grass that is renewed in the morning:
6 in the morning it flourishes and is renewed;
  in the evening it fades and withers.

7 For we are brought to an end by your anger;
  by your wrath we are dismayed.
8 You have set our iniquities before you,
  our secret sins in the light of your presence.

Reflection

AUGUST 12
~ Psalm 90:9-17

9   For all our days pass away under your wrath;
        we bring our years to an end like a sigh.

10   The years of our life are seventy,
        or even by reason of strength eighty;
    yet their span is but toil and trouble;
        they are soon gone, and we fly away.

11   Who considers the power of your anger,
        and your wrath according to the fear of you?

12   So teach us to number our days
        that we may get a heart of wisdom.

13   Return, O LORD! How long?
        Have pity on your servants!

14   Satisfy us in the morning with your steadfast love,
        that we may rejoice and be glad all our days.

15   Make us glad for as many days as you have afflicted us,
        and for as many years as we have seen evil.

16   Let your work be shown to your servants,
        and your glorious power to their children.

17   Let the favor of the Lord our God be upon us,
        and establish the work of our hands upon us;
        yes, establish the work of our hands!

Reflection

AUGUST 13
~ Psalm 91:1-8

My Refuge and My Fortress

91

1 He who dwells in the shelter of the Most High
   will abide in the shadow of the Almighty.
2 I will say to the LORD, "My refuge and my fortress,
   my God, in whom I trust."

3 For he will deliver you from the snare of the fowler
   and from the deadly pestilence.
4 He will cover you with his pinions,
   and under his wings you will find refuge;
   his faithfulness is a shield and buckler.
5 You will not fear the terror of the night,
   nor the arrow that flies by day,
6 nor the pestilence that stalks in darkness,
   nor the destruction that wastes at noonday.

7 A thousand may fall at your side,
   ten thousand at your right hand,
   but it will not come near you.
8 You will only look with your eyes
   and see the recompense of the wicked.

Reflection

_____

_____

_____

_____

_____

Satisfy us
in the morning
with your
steadfast love,
that we may
rejoice
& be glad
all our days.
Psalm 90:14

AUGUST 14
~ Psalm 91:9-16

9 Because you have made the LORD your dwelling place—
     the Most High, who is my refuge—
10 no evil shall be allowed to befall you,
     no plague come near your tent.

11 For he will command his angels concerning you
     to guard you in all your ways.
12 On their hands they will bear you up,
     lest you strike your foot against a stone.
13 You will tread on the lion and the adder;
     the young lion and the serpent you will
       trample underfoot.

14 "Because he holds fast to me in love, I will deliver him;
     I will protect him, because he knows my name.
15 When he calls to me, I will answer him;
     I will be with him in trouble;
     I will rescue him and honor him.
16 With long life I will satisfy him
     and show him my salvation."

Reflection

AUGUST 15
~ Psalm 92:1-9

How Great Are Your Works

A Psalm. A Song for the Sabbath.

1 It is good to give thanks to the LORD,
    to sing praises to your name, O Most High;
2 to declare your steadfast love in the morning,
    and your faithfulness by night,
3 to the music of the lute and the harp,
    to the melody of the lyre.
4 For you, O LORD, have made me glad by your work;
    at the works of your hands I sing for joy.

5 How great are your works, O LORD!
    Your thoughts are very deep!
6 The stupid man cannot know;
    the fool cannot understand this:
7 that though the wicked sprout like grass
    and all evildoers flourish,
    they are doomed to destruction forever;
8 but you, O LORD, are on high forever.
9 For behold, your enemies, O LORD,
    for behold, your enemies shall perish;
    all evildoers shall be scattered.

Reflection

AUGUST 16
~ Psalm 92:10-15

10   But you have exalted my horn like that of the wild ox;
        you have poured over me fresh oil.

11   My eyes have seen the downfall of my enemies;
        my ears have heard the doom of my evil assailants.

12   The righteous flourish like the palm tree
        and grow like a cedar in Lebanon.

13   They are planted in the house of the LORD;
        they flourish in the courts of our God.

14   They still bear fruit in old age;
        they are ever full of sap and green,

15   to declare that the LORD is upright;
        he is my rock, and there is no unrighteousness in him.

Reflection

AUGUST 17
~ Psalm 93

The LORD Reigns

1 The LORD reigns; he is robed in majesty;
   the LORD is robed; he has put on strength as his belt.
   Yes, the world is established; it shall never be moved.
2 Your throne is established from of old;
   you are from everlasting.

3 The floods have lifted up, O LORD,
   the floods have lifted up their voice;
   the floods lift up their roaring.
4 Mightier than the thunders of many waters,
   mightier than the waves of the sea,
   the LORD on high is mighty!

5 Your decrees are very trustworthy;
   holiness befits your house,
   O LORD, forevermore.

Reflection

AUGUST 18
~ Psalm 94:1-7

The Lord Will Not Forsake His People

1. O LORD, God of vengeance,
   O God of vengeance, shine forth!
2. Rise up, O judge of the earth;
   repay to the proud what they deserve!
3. O LORD, how long shall the wicked,
   how long shall the wicked exult?
4. They pour out their arrogant words;
   all the evildoers boast.
5. They crush your people, O LORD,
   and afflict your heritage.
6. They kill the widow and the sojourner,
   and murder the fatherless;
7. and they say, "The LORD does not see;
   the God of Jacob does not perceive."

Reflection

AUGUST 19
~ Psalm 94:8-15

8   Understand, O dullest of the people!
       Fools, when will you be wise?
9   He who planted the ear, does he not hear?
       He who formed the eye, does he not see?
10   He who disciplines the nations, does he not rebuke?
       He who teaches man knowledge—
11   the LORD—knows the thoughts of man,
       that they are but a breath.

12   Blessed is the man whom you discipline, O LORD,
       and whom you teach out of your law,
13   to give him rest from days of trouble,
       until a pit is dug for the wicked.
14   For the LORD will not forsake his people;
       he will not abandon his heritage;
15   for justice will return to the righteous,
       and all the upright in heart will follow it.

Reflection

AUGUST 20
~ Psalm 94:16-23

16   Who rises up for me against the wicked?
      Who stands up for me against evildoers?

17   If the LORD had not been my help,
      my soul would soon have lived in the land of silence.

18   When I thought, "My foot slips,"
      your steadfast love, O LORD, held me up.

19   When the cares of my heart are many,
      your consolations cheer my soul.

20   Can wicked rulers be allied with you,
      those who frame injustice by statute?

21   They band together against the life of the righteous
      and condemn the innocent to death.

22   But the LORD has become my stronghold,
      and my God the rock of my refuge.

23   He will bring back on them their iniquity
      and wipe them out for their wickedness;
      the LORD our God will wipe them out.

Reflection

Mightier
than the thunders of many *waters,*
mightier than the
waves of the sea,
the LORD
on high is
mighty!

Psalm 93:4

AUGUST 21
~ Psalm 95:1-5

Let Us *Sing Songs of Praise*

1 Oh come, let us sing to the LORD;
    let us make a joyful noise to the rock of our salvation!
2 Let us come into his presence with thanksgiving;
    let us make a joyful noise to him with songs of praise!
3 For the LORD is a great God,
    and a great King above all gods.
4 In his hand are the depths of the earth;
    the heights of the mountains are his also.
5 The sea is his, for he made it,
    and his hands formed the dry land.

Reflection

_____
_____
_____
_____
_____
_____
_____
_____
_____
_____
_____

AUGUST 22
~ Psalm 95:6-11

6   Oh come, let us worship and bow down;
        let us kneel before the LORD, our Maker!

7   For he is our God,
        and we are the people of his pasture,
        and the sheep of his hand.
    Today, if you hear his voice,

8   do not harden your hearts, as at Meribah,
        as on the day at Massah in the wilderness,

9   when your fathers put me to the test
        and put me to the proof, though they had seen my work.

10   For forty years I loathed that generation
        and said, "They are a people who go astray in their heart,
        and they have not known my ways."

11   Therefore I swore in my wrath,
        "They shall not enter my rest."

AUGUST 23
~ Psalm 96:1-6

Worship in the Splendor of Holiness

1   Oh sing to the LORD a new song;
     sing to the LORD, all the earth!

2   Sing to the LORD, bless his name;
     tell of his salvation from day to day.

3   Declare his glory among the nations,
     his marvelous works among all the peoples!

4   For great is the LORD, and greatly to be praised;
     he is to be feared above all gods.

5   For all the gods of the peoples are worthless idols,
     but the LORD made the heavens.

6   Splendor and majesty are before him;
     strength and beauty are in his sanctuary.

Reflection

AUGUST 24
~ Psalm 96:7-13

7   Ascribe to the LORD, O families of the peoples,
        ascribe to the LORD glory and strength!
8   Ascribe to the LORD the glory due his name;
        bring an offering, and come into his courts!
9   Worship the LORD in the splendor of holiness;
        tremble before him, all the earth!

10   Say among the nations, "The LORD reigns!
        Yes, the world is established; it shall never be moved;
        he will judge the peoples with equity."

11   Let the heavens be glad, and let the earth rejoice;
        let the sea roar, and all that fills it;
12   let the field exult, and everything in it!
     Then shall all the trees of the forest sing for joy
13   before the LORD, for he comes,
        for he comes to judge the earth.
     He will judge the world in righteousness,
        and the peoples in his faithfulness.

Reflection

AUGUST 25
~ Psalm 97:1-6

The Lord Reigns

1 The LORD reigns, let the earth rejoice;
  let the many coastlands be glad!
2 Clouds and thick darkness are all around him;
  righteousness and justice are the foundation
    of his throne.
3 Fire goes before him
  and burns up his adversaries all around.
4 His lightnings light up the world;
  the earth sees and trembles.
5 The mountains melt like wax before the LORD,
  before the Lord of all the earth.

6 The heavens proclaim his righteousness,
  and all the peoples see his glory.

Reflection

AUGUST 26
~ Psalm 97:7-12

7   All worshipers of images are put to shame,
      who make their boast in worthless idols;
      worship him, all you gods!

8   Zion hears and is glad,
      and the daughters of Judah rejoice,
      because of your judgments, O Lord.

9   For you, O Lord, are most high over all the earth;
      you are exalted far above all gods.

10   O you who love the Lord, hate evil!
      He preserves the lives of his saints;
      he delivers them from the hand of the wicked.

11   Light is sown for the righteous,
      and joy for the upright in heart.

12   Rejoice in the Lord, O you righteous,
      and give thanks to his holy name!

Reflection

AUGUST 27
~ Psalm 98

Make a *Joyful Noise* to the LORD

A Psalm.

1   Oh sing to the LORD a new song,
     for he has done marvelous things!
   His right hand and his holy arm
     have worked salvation for him.
2   The LORD has made known his salvation;
     he has revealed his righteousness in the sight
       of the nations.
3   He has remembered his steadfast love and faithfulness
     to the house of Israel.
   All the ends of the earth have seen
     the salvation of our God.

4   Make a joyful noise to the LORD, all the earth;
     break forth into joyous song and sing praises!
5   Sing praises to the LORD with the lyre,
     with the lyre and the sound of melody!
6   With trumpets and the sound of the horn
     make a joyful noise before the King, the LORD!

7   Let the sea roar, and all that fills it;
     the world and those who dwell in it!
8   Let the rivers clap their hands;
     let the hills sing for joy together
9   before the LORD, for he comes
     to judge the earth.
   He will judge the world with righteousness,
     and the peoples with equity.

Oh sing to the LORD a new song; sing to the Lord, all the earth! *Psalm 96:1*

AUGUST 28
~ Psalm 99

The Lord Our God Is Holy

1 The Lord reigns; let the peoples tremble!
   He sits enthroned upon the cherubim; let the earth quake!
2 The Lord is great in Zion;
   he is exalted over all the peoples.
3 Let them praise your great and awesome name!
   Holy is he!
4 The King in his might loves justice.
   You have established equity;
you have executed justice
   and righteousness in Jacob.
5 Exalt the Lord our God;
   worship at his footstool!
   Holy is he!

6 Moses and Aaron were among his priests,
   Samuel also was among those who called upon his name.
   They called to the Lord, and he answered them.
7 In the pillar of the cloud he spoke to them;
   they kept his testimonies
   and the statute that he gave them.

8 O Lord our God, you answered them;
   you were a forgiving God to them,
   but an avenger of their wrongdoings.
9 Exalt the Lord our God,
   and worship at his holy mountain;
   for the Lord our God is holy!

AUGUST 29

~ Psalm 100

His Steadfast Love Endures Forever

A Psalm for giving thanks.

1 Make a joyful noise to the LORD, all the earth!
2   Serve the LORD with gladness!
       Come into his presence with singing!

3 Know that the LORD, he is God!
       It is he who made us, and we are his;
       we are his people, and the sheep of his pasture.

4 Enter his gates with thanksgiving,
       and his courts with praise!
       Give thanks to him; bless his name!

5 For the LORD is good;
       his steadfast love endures forever,
       and his faithfulness to all generations.

Reflection

AUGUST 30
~ Psalm 101

I Will Walk with *Integrity*

A Psalm of David.

1   I will sing of steadfast love and justice;
    to you, O LORD, I will make music.
2   I will ponder the way that is blameless.
    Oh when will you come to me?
    I will walk with integrity of heart
    within my house;
3   I will not set before my eyes
    anything that is worthless.
    I hate the work of those who fall away;
    it shall not cling to me.
4   A perverse heart shall be far from me;
    I will know nothing of evil.

5   Whoever slanders his neighbor secretly
    I will destroy.
    Whoever has a haughty look and an arrogant heart
    I will not endure.

6 I will look with favor on the faithful in the land,
       that they may dwell with me;
   he who walks in the way that is blameless
       shall minister to me.

7 No one who practices deceit
       shall dwell in my house;
   no one who utters lies
       shall continue before my eyes.

8 Morning by morning I will destroy
       all the wicked in the land,
   cutting off all the evildoers
       from the city of the LORD.

Reflection

AUGUST 31
~ Psalm 102:1-7

Do Not Hide Your Face from Me

A Prayer of one afflicted, when he is faint and pours out his complaint before the LORD.

1 Hear my prayer, O LORD;
  let my cry come to you!
2 Do not hide your face from me
    in the day of my distress!
  Incline your ear to me;
    answer me speedily in the day when I call!

3 For my days pass away like smoke,
    and my bones burn like a furnace.
4 My heart is struck down like grass and has withered;
    I forget to eat my bread.
5 Because of my loud groaning
    my bones cling to my flesh.
6 I am like a desert owl of the wilderness,
    like an owl of the waste places;
7 I lie awake;
    I am like a lonely sparrow on the housetop.

Reflection

SEPTEMBER 1
~ Psalm 102:8-15

8   All the day my enemies taunt me;
       those who deride me use my name for a curse.

9   For I eat ashes like bread
       and mingle tears with my drink,

10   because of your indignation and anger;
       for you have taken me up and thrown me down.

11   My days are like an evening shadow;
       I wither away like grass.

12   But you, O Lord, are enthroned forever;
       you are remembered throughout all generations.

13   You will arise and have pity on Zion;
       it is the time to favor her;
       the appointed time has come.

14   For your servants hold her stones dear
       and have pity on her dust.

15   Nations will fear the name of the Lord,
       and all the kings of the earth will fear your glory.

Reflection

SEPTEMBER 2
~ Psalm 102:16-22

16   For the Lord builds up Zion;
        he appears in his glory;
17   he regards the prayer of the destitute
        and does not despise their prayer.

18   Let this be recorded for a generation to come,
        so that a people yet to be created may praise the Lord:
19   that he looked down from his holy height;
        from heaven the Lord looked at the earth,
20   to hear the groans of the prisoners,
        to set free those who were doomed to die,
21   that they may declare in Zion the name of the Lord,
        and in Jerusalem his praise,
22   when peoples gather together,
        and kingdoms, to worship the Lord.

Reflection

SEPTEMBER 3
~ Psalm 102:23-28

23   He has broken my strength in midcourse;
        he has shortened my days.

24   " O my God," I say, "take me not away
        in the midst of my days—
    you whose years endure
        throughout all generations!"

25   Of old you laid the foundation of the earth,
        and the heavens are the work of your hands.

26   They will perish, but you will remain;
        they will all wear out like a garment.
    You will change them like a robe, and they will pass away,

27   but you are the same, and your years have no end.

28   The children of your servants shall dwell secure;
        their offspring shall be established before you.

Reflection

For the LORD is good;
his steadfast love
endures forever,
and his *faithfulness* to all generations.

Psalm 100:5

SEPTEMBER 4
~ Psalm 103:1-7

Bless the Lord, O My Soul

Of David.

1 Bless the LORD, O my soul,
    and all that is within me,
    bless his holy name!
2 Bless the LORD, O my soul,
    and forget not all his benefits,
3 who forgives all your iniquity,
    who heals all your diseases,
4 who redeems your life from the pit,
    who crowns you with steadfast love and mercy,
5 who satisfies you with good
    so that your youth is renewed like the eagle's.

6 The LORD works righteousness
    and justice for all who are oppressed.
7 He made known his ways to Moses,
    his acts to the people of Israel.

Reflection

SEPTEMBER 5
~ Psalm 103:8-14

8   The LORD is merciful and gracious,
      slow to anger and abounding in steadfast love.

9   He will not always chide,
      nor will he keep his anger forever.

10   He does not deal with us according to our sins,
      nor repay us according to our iniquities.

11   For as high as the heavens are above the earth,
      so great is his steadfast love toward those who fear him;

12   as far as the east is from the west,
      so far does he remove our transgressions from us.

13   As a father shows compassion to his children,
      so the LORD shows compassion to those who fear him.

14   For he knows our frame;
      he remembers that we are dust.

Reflection

SEPTEMBER 6
~ Psalm 103:15-22

15   As for man, his days are like grass;
        he flourishes like a flower of the field;
16   for the wind passes over it, and it is gone,
        and its place knows it no more.
17   But the steadfast love of the LORD is from everlasting to
        everlasting on those who fear him,
        and his righteousness to children's children,
18   to those who keep his covenant
        and remember to do his commandments.
19   The LORD has established his throne in the heavens,
        and his kingdom rules over all.

20   Bless the LORD, O you his angels,
        you mighty ones who do his word,
        obeying the voice of his word!
21   Bless the LORD, all his hosts,
        his ministers, who do his will!
22   Bless the LORD, all his works,
        in all places of his dominion.
    Bless the LORD, O my soul!

Reflection

SEPTEMBER 7
~ Psalm 104:1-7

O Lord My God, You Are Very Great

1 Bless the LORD, O my soul!
 O LORD my God, you are very great!
 You are clothed with splendor and majesty,
2 covering yourself with light as with a garment,
 stretching out the heavens like a tent.
3 He lays the beams of his chambers on the waters;
 he makes the clouds his chariot;
 he rides on the wings of the wind;
4 he makes his messengers winds,
 his ministers a flaming fire.

5 He set the earth on its foundations,
 so that it should never be moved.
6 You covered it with the deep as with a garment;
 the waters stood above the mountains.
7 At your rebuke they fled;
 at the sound of your thunder they took to flight.

Reflection

SEPTEMBER 8
~ Psalm 104:8-13

8   The mountains rose, the valleys sank down
       to the place that you appointed for them.
9   You set a boundary that they may not pass,
       so that they might not again cover the earth.

10   You make springs gush forth in the valleys;
       they flow between the hills;
11   they give drink to every beast of the field;
       the wild donkeys quench their thirst.
12   Beside them the birds of the heavens dwell;
       they sing among the branches.
13   From your lofty abode you water the mountains;
       the earth is satisfied with the fruit of your work.

SEPTEMBER 9
~ Psalm 104:14-20

14   You cause the grass to grow for the livestock
       and plants for man to cultivate,
    that he may bring forth food from the earth
15   and wine to gladden the heart of man,
    oil to make his face shine
       and bread to strengthen man's heart.

16   The trees of the LORD are watered abundantly,
       the cedars of Lebanon that he planted.
17   In them the birds build their nests;
       the stork has her home in the fir trees.
18   The high mountains are for the wild goats;
       the rocks are a refuge for the rock badgers.

19   He made the moon to mark the seasons;
       the sun knows its time for setting.
20   You make darkness, and it is night,
       when all the beasts of the forest creep about.

Reflection

SEPTEMBER 10
~ Psalm 104:21-26

21 The young lions roar for their prey,
    seeking their food from God.
22 When the sun rises, they steal away
    and lie down in their dens.
23 Man goes out to his work
    and to his labor until the evening.

24 O LORD, how manifold are your works!
    In wisdom have you made them all;
    the earth is full of your creatures.
25 Here is the sea, great and wide,
    which teems with creatures innumerable,
    living things both small and great.
26 There go the ships,
    and Leviathan, which you formed to play in it.

Reflection

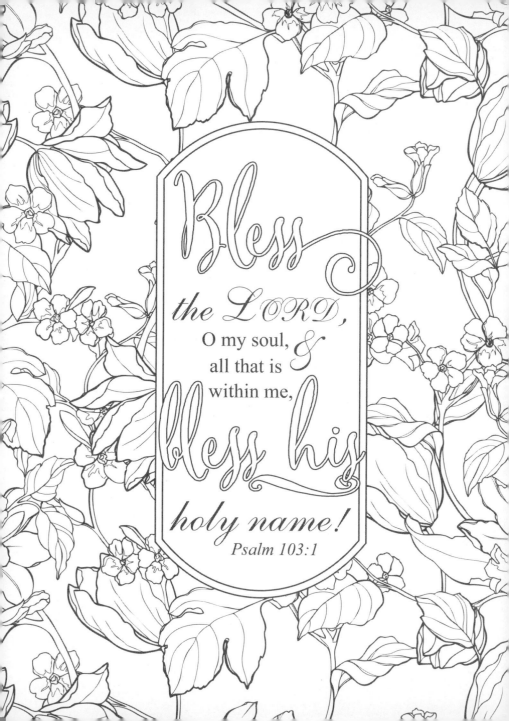

Bless the LORD, O my soul, & all that is within me, bless his holy name!

Psalm 103:1

SEPTEMBER 11
~ Psalm 104:27-35

27 These all look to you,
   to give them their food in due season.
28 When you give it to them, they gather it up;
   when you open your hand, they are filled with good things.
29 When you hide your face, they are dismayed;
   when you take away their breath, they die
   and return to their dust.
30 When you send forth your Spirit, they are created,
   and you renew the face of the ground.

31 May the glory of the LORD endure forever;
   may the LORD rejoice in his works,
32 who looks on the earth and it trembles,
   who touches the mountains and they smoke!
33 I will sing to the LORD as long as I live;
   I will sing praise to my God while I have being.
34 May my meditation be pleasing to him,
   for I rejoice in the LORD.
35 Let sinners be consumed from the earth,
   and let the wicked be no more!
   Bless the LORD, O my soul!
   Praise the LORD!

Reflection

SEPTEMBER 12
~ Psalm 105:1-7

Tell of All His *Wondrous Works*

1 Oh give thanks to the LORD; call upon his name;
   make known his deeds among the peoples!

2 Sing to him, sing praises to him;
   tell of all his wondrous works!

3 Glory in his holy name;
   let the hearts of those who seek the LORD rejoice!

4 Seek the LORD and his strength;
   seek his presence continually!

5 Remember the wondrous works that he has done,
   his miracles, and the judgments he uttered,

6 O offspring of Abraham, his servant,
   children of Jacob, his chosen ones!

7 He is the LORD our God;
   his judgments are in all the earth.

Reflection

SEPTEMBER 13
~ Psalm 105:8-15

8   He remembers his covenant forever,
      the word that he commanded, for a thousand generations,

9   the covenant that he made with Abraham,
      his sworn promise to Isaac,

10   which he confirmed to Jacob as a statute,
      to Israel as an everlasting covenant,

11   saying, "To you I will give the land of Canaan
      as your portion for an inheritance."

12   When they were few in number,
      of little account, and sojourners in it,

13   wandering from nation to nation,
      from one kingdom to another people,

14   he allowed no one to oppress them;
      he rebuked kings on their account,

15   saying, "Touch not my anointed ones,
      do my prophets no harm!"

Reflection

SEPTEMBER 14
~ Psalm 105:16-22

16   When he summoned a famine on the land
       and broke all supply of bread,

17   he had sent a man ahead of them,
       Joseph, who was sold as a slave.

18   His feet were hurt with fetters;
       his neck was put in a collar of iron;

19   until what he had said came to pass,
       the word of the Lord tested him.

20   The king sent and released him;
       the ruler of the peoples set him free;

21   he made him lord of his house
       and ruler of all his possessions,

22   to bind his princes at his pleasure
       and to teach his elders wisdom.

Reflection

SEPTEMBER 15
~ Psalm 105:23-30

23 Then Israel came to Egypt;
    Jacob sojourned in the land of Ham.
24 And the Lord made his people very fruitful
    and made them stronger than their foes.
25 He turned their hearts to hate his people,
    to deal craftily with his servants.

26 He sent Moses, his servant,
    and Aaron, whom he had chosen.
27 They performed his signs among them
    and miracles in the land of Ham.
28 He sent darkness, and made the land dark;
    they did not rebel against his words.
29 He turned their waters into blood
    and caused their fish to die.
30 Their land swarmed with frogs,
    even in the chambers of their kings.

Reflection

SEPTEMBER 16
~ Psalm 105:31-37

31 He spoke, and there came swarms of flies,
   and gnats throughout their country.
32 He gave them hail for rain,
   and fiery lightning bolts through their land.
33 He struck down their vines and fig trees,
   and shattered the trees of their country.
34 He spoke, and the locusts came,
   young locusts without number,
35 which devoured all the vegetation in their land
   and ate up the fruit of their ground.
36 He struck down all the firstborn in their land,
   the firstfruits of all their strength.

37 Then he brought out Israel with silver and gold,
   and there was none among his tribes who stumbled.

Reflection

SEPTEMBER 17
~ Psalm 105:38-45

38   Egypt was glad when they departed,
      for dread of them had fallen upon it.

39   He spread a cloud for a covering,
      and fire to give light by night.

40   They asked, and he brought quail,
      and gave them bread from heaven in abundance.

41   He opened the rock, and water gushed out;
      it flowed through the desert like a river.

42   For he remembered his holy promise,
      and Abraham, his servant.

43   So he brought his people out with joy,
      his chosen ones with singing.

44   And he gave them the lands of the nations,
      and they took possession of the fruit of the peoples' toil,

45   that they might keep his statutes
      and observe his laws.
      Praise the LORD!

Reflection

I will sing to the Lord as long as I live;
I will sing praise to my God while I have being.

Psalm 104:33

SEPTEMBER 18

~ Psalm 106:1-8

Give Thanks to the LORD, for He Is Good

1 Praise the LORD!
Oh give thanks to the LORD, for he is good,
   for his steadfast love endures forever!
2 Who can utter the mighty deeds of the LORD,
   or declare all his praise?
3 Blessed are they who observe justice,
   who do righteousness at all times!

4 Remember me, O LORD, when you show favor to your people;
   help me when you save them,
5 that I may look upon the prosperity of your chosen ones,
   that I may rejoice in the gladness of your nation,
   that I may glory with your inheritance.

6 Both we and our fathers have sinned;
   we have committed iniquity; we have done wickedness.
7 Our fathers, when they were in Egypt,
   did not consider your wondrous works;
   they did not remember the abundance of your steadfast love,
   but rebelled by the sea, at the Red Sea.
8 Yet he saved them for his name's sake,
   that he might make known his mighty power.

Reflection

SEPTEMBER 19
~ Psalm 106:9-15

9   He rebuked the Red Sea, and it became dry,
        and he led them through the deep as through a desert.

10   So he saved them from the hand of the foe
        and redeemed them from the power of the enemy.

11   And the waters covered their adversaries;
        not one of them was left.

12   Then they believed his words;
        they sang his praise.

13   But they soon forgot his works;
        they did not wait for his counsel.

14   But they had a wanton craving in the wilderness,
        and put God to the test in the desert;

15   he gave them what they asked,
        but sent a wasting disease among them.

Reflection

SEPTEMBER 20
~ Psalm 106:16-24

16   When men in the camp were jealous of Moses
        and Aaron, the holy one of the LORD,

17   the earth opened and swallowed up Dathan,
        and covered the company of Abiram.

18   Fire also broke out in their company;
        the flame burned up the wicked.

19   They made a calf in Horeb
        and worshiped a metal image.

20   They exchanged the glory of God
        for the image of an ox that eats grass.

21   They forgot God, their Savior,
        who had done great things in Egypt,

22   wondrous works in the land of Ham,
        and awesome deeds by the Red Sea.

23   Therefore he said he would destroy them—
        had not Moses, his chosen one,
    stood in the breach before him,
        to turn away his wrath from destroying them.

24   Then they despised the pleasant land,
        having no faith in his promise.

Reflection

SEPTEMBER 21
~ Psalm 106:25-31

25 They murmured in their tents,
     and did not obey the voice of the LORD.
26 Therefore he raised his hand and swore to them
     that he would make them fall in the wilderness,
27 and would make their offspring fall among the nations,
     scattering them among the lands.

28 Then they yoked themselves to the Baal of Peor,
     and ate sacrifices offered to the dead;
29 they provoked the LORD to anger with their deeds,
     and a plague broke out among them.
30 Then Phinehas stood up and intervened,
     and the plague was stayed.
31 And that was counted to him as righteousness
     from generation to generation forever.

Reflection

_____
_____
_____
_____
_____
_____
_____
_____
_____
_____
_____

SEPTEMBER 22
~ Psalm 106:32-41

32 They angered him at the waters of Meribah,
  and it went ill with Moses on their account,
33 for they made his spirit bitter,
  and he spoke rashly with his lips.

34 They did not destroy the peoples,
  as the LORD commanded them,
35 but they mixed with the nations
  and learned to do as they did.
36 They served their idols,
  which became a snare to them.
37 They sacrificed their sons
  and their daughters to the demons;
38 they poured out innocent blood,
  the blood of their sons and daughters,
whom they sacrificed to the idols of Canaan,
  and the land was polluted with blood.
39 Thus they became unclean by their acts,
  and played the whore in their deeds.

40 Then the anger of the LORD was kindled against his people,
  and he abhorred his heritage;
41 he gave them into the hand of the nations,
  so that those who hated them ruled over them.

Reflection

SEPTEMBER 23
~ Psalm 106:42-48

42 Their enemies oppressed them,
   and they were brought into subjection under their power.
43 Many times he delivered them,
   but they were rebellious in their purposes
   and were brought low through their iniquity.

44 Nevertheless, he looked upon their distress,
   when he heard their cry.
45 For their sake he remembered his covenant,
   and relented according to the abundance of
      his steadfast love.
46 He caused them to be pitied
   by all those who held them captive.

47 Save us, O LORD our God,
   and gather us from among the nations,
   that we may give thanks to your holy name
   and glory in your praise.

48 Blessed be the LORD, the God of Israel,
   from everlasting to everlasting!
   And let all the people say, "Amen!"
   Praise the LORD!

Reflection

SEPTEMBER 24
~ Psalm 107:1-7

Let the of the LORD Say So

1 Oh give thanks to the LORD, for he is good,
   for his steadfast love endures forever!
2 Let the redeemed of the LORD say so,
   whom he has redeemed from trouble
3 and gathered in from the lands,
   from the east and from the west,
   from the north and from the south.

4 Some wandered in desert wastes,
   finding no way to a city to dwell in;
5 hungry and thirsty,
   their soul fainted within them.
6 Then they cried to the LORD in their trouble,
   and he delivered them from their distress.
7 He led them by a straight way
   till they reached a city to dwell in.

Reflection

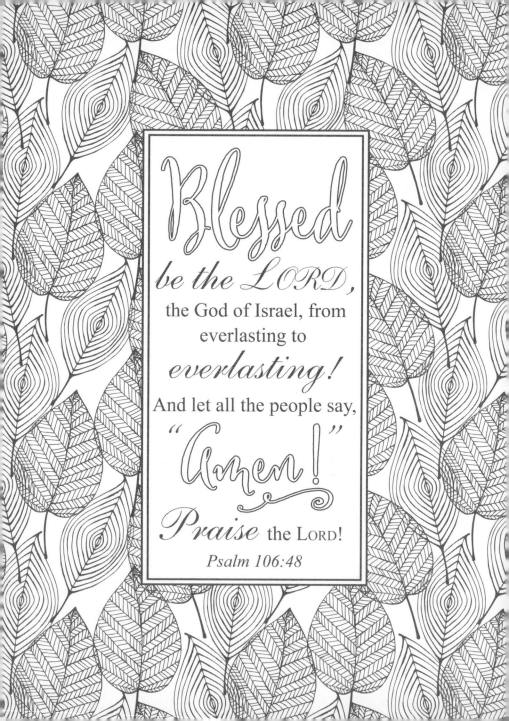

Blessed
be the LORD,
the God of Israel, from
everlasting to
everlasting!
And let all the people say,
"Amen!"
Praise the LORD!
Psalm 106:48

SEPTEMBER 25
~ Psalm 107:8-14

8   Let them thank the LORD for his steadfast love,
        for his wondrous works to the children of man!

9   For he satisfies the longing soul,
        and the hungry soul he fills with good things.

10   Some sat in darkness and in the shadow of death,
        prisoners in affliction and in irons,

11   for they had rebelled against the words of God,
        and spurned the counsel of the Most High.

12   So he bowed their hearts down with hard labor;
        they fell down, with none to help.

13   Then they cried to the LORD in their trouble,
        and he delivered them from their distress.

14   He brought them out of darkness and the shadow of death,
        and burst their bonds apart.

Reflection

SEPTEMBER 26
~ Psalm 107:15-20

15   Let them thank the Lord for his steadfast love,
      for his wondrous works to the children of man!

16   For he shatters the doors of bronze
      and cuts in two the bars of iron.

17   Some were fools through their sinful ways,
      and because of their iniquities suffered affliction;

18   they loathed any kind of food,
      and they drew near to the gates of death.

19   Then they cried to the Lord in their trouble,
      and he delivered them from their distress.

20   He sent out his word and healed them,
      and delivered them from their destruction.

Reflection

SEPTEMBER 27
~ Psalm 107:21-28

21   Let them thank the LORD for his steadfast love,
        for his wondrous works to the children of man!

22   And let them offer sacrifices of thanksgiving,
        and tell of his deeds in songs of joy!

23   Some went down to the sea in ships,
        doing business on the great waters;

24   they saw the deeds of the LORD,
        his wondrous works in the deep.

25   For he commanded and raised the stormy wind,
        which lifted up the waves of the sea.

26   They mounted up to heaven; they went down to the depths;
        their courage melted away in their evil plight;

27   they reeled and staggered like drunken men
        and were at their wits' end.

28   Then they cried to the LORD in their trouble,
        and he delivered them from their distress.

Reflection

SEPTEMBER 28
~ Psalm 107:29-35

29 He made the storm be still,
    and the waves of the sea were hushed.
30 Then they were glad that the waters were quiet,
    and he brought them to their desired haven.
31 Let them thank the LORD for his steadfast love,
    for his wondrous works to the children of man!
32 Let them extol him in the congregation of the people,
    and praise him in the assembly of the elders.

33 He turns rivers into a desert,
    springs of water into thirsty ground,
34 a fruitful land into a salty waste,
    because of the evil of its inhabitants.
35 He turns a desert into pools of water,
    a parched land into springs of water.

Reflection

SEPTEMBER 29
~ Psalm 107:36-43

36   And there he lets the hungry dwell,
      and they establish a city to live in;
37   they sow fields and plant vineyards
      and get a fruitful yield.
38   By his blessing they multiply greatly,
      and he does not let their livestock diminish.

39   When they are diminished and brought low
      through oppression, evil, and sorrow,
40   he pours contempt on princes
      and makes them wander in trackless wastes;
41   but he raises up the needy out of affliction
      and makes their families like flocks.
42   The upright see it and are glad,
      and all wickedness shuts its mouth.

43   Whoever is wise, let him attend to these things;
      let them consider the steadfast love of the LORD.

Reflection

SEPTEMBER 30
~ Psalm 108:1-6

With God We Shall Do *Valiantly*

A Song. A Psalm of David.

1 My heart is steadfast, O God!
   I will sing and make melody with all my being!
2 Awake, O harp and lyre!
   I will awake the dawn!
3 I will give thanks to you, O LORD, among the peoples;
   I will sing praises to you among the nations.
4 For your steadfast love is great above the heavens;
   your faithfulness reaches to the clouds.

5 Be exalted, O God, above the heavens!
   Let your glory be over all the earth!
6 That your beloved ones may be delivered,
   give salvation by your right hand and answer me!

Reflection

OCTOBER 1
~ Psalm 108:7-13

7   God has promised in his holiness:
       "With exultation I will divide up Shechem
       and portion out the Valley of Succoth.
8   Gilead is mine; Manasseh is mine;
       Ephraim is my helmet,
       Judah my scepter.
9   Moab is my washbasin;
       upon Edom I cast my shoe;
       over Philistia I shout in triumph."

10   Who will bring me to the fortified city?
       Who will lead me to Edom?
11   Have you not rejected us, O God?
       You do not go out, O God, with our armies.
12   Oh grant us help against the foe,
       for vain is the salvation of man!
13   With God we shall do valiantly;
       it is he who will tread down our foes.

Reflection

Let them thank *the LORD* *love,* for his *steadfast* for his *wondrous works* to the children of man! *For he satisfies* the longing soul, & the hungry soul he fills with *good* *things.*

Psalm 107:8-9

OCTOBER 2
~ Psalm 109:1-6

Help Me, O LORD *My God*

To the choirmaster. A Psalm of David.

1 Be not silent, O God of my praise!
2 For wicked and deceitful mouths are opened against me,
    speaking against me with lying tongues.
3 They encircle me with words of hate,
    and attack me without cause.
4 In return for my love they accuse me,
    but I give myself to prayer.
5 So they reward me evil for good,
    and hatred for my love.

6 Appoint a wicked man against him;
    let an accuser stand at his right hand.

Reflection

OCTOBER 3
~ Psalm 109:7-12

7   When he is tried, let him come forth guilty;
       let his prayer be counted as sin!
8   May his days be few;
       may another take his office!
9   May his children be fatherless
       and his wife a widow!
10   May his children wander about and beg,
       seeking food far from the ruins they inhabit!
11   May the creditor seize all that he has;
       may strangers plunder the fruits of his toil!
12   Let there be none to extend kindness to him,
       nor any to pity his fatherless children!

Reflection

_____
_____
_____
_____
_____
_____
_____
_____
_____
_____

OCTOBER 4
~ Psalm 109:13-18

13   May his posterity be cut off;
        may his name be blotted out in the second generation!
14   May the iniquity of his fathers be remembered before
        the LORD,
        and let not the sin of his mother be blotted out!
15   Let them be before the LORD continually,
        that he may cut off the memory of them from the earth!

16   For he did not remember to show kindness,
        but pursued the poor and needy
        and the brokenhearted, to put them to death.
17   He loved to curse; let curses come upon him!
        He did not delight in blessing; may it be far from him!
18   He clothed himself with cursing as his coat;
        may it soak into his body like water,
        like oil into his bones!

Reflection

OCTOBER 5
~ Psalm 109:19-25

19   May it be like a garment that he wraps around him,
      like a belt that he puts on every day!

20   May this be the reward of my accusers from the LORD,
      of those who speak evil against my life!

21   But you, O GOD my Lord,
      deal on my behalf for your name's sake;
      because your steadfast love is good, deliver me!

22   For I am poor and needy,
      and my heart is stricken within me.

23   I am gone like a shadow at evening;
      I am shaken off like a locust.

24   My knees are weak through fasting;
      my body has become gaunt, with no fat.

25   I am an object of scorn to my accusers;
      when they see me, they wag their heads.

Reflection

OCTOBER 6
~ Psalm 109:26-31

26   Help me, O Lord my God!
       Save me according to your steadfast love!

27   Let them know that this is your hand;
       you, O Lord, have done it!

28   Let them curse, but you will bless!
       They arise and are put to shame, but your servant
          will be glad!

29   May my accusers be clothed with dishonor;
       may they be wrapped in their own shame as in a cloak!

30   With my mouth I will give great thanks to the Lord;
       I will praise him in the midst of the throng.

31   For he stands at the right hand of the needy one,
       to save him from those who condemn his soul to death.

Reflection

OCTOBER 7
~ Psalm 110

Sit at My Right Hand

A Psalm of David.

1 The LORD says to my Lord:
   "Sit at my right hand,
until I make your enemies your footstool."

2 The LORD sends forth from Zion
      your mighty scepter.
      Rule in the midst of your enemies!

3 Your people will offer themselves freely
      on the day of your power,
      in holy garments;
   from the womb of the morning,
      the dew of your youth will be yours.

4 The LORD has sworn
      and will not change his mind,
   "You are a priest forever
      after the order of Melchizedek."

5 The Lord is at your right hand;
      he will shatter kings on the day of his wrath.

6 He will execute judgment among the nations,
      filling them with corpses;
   he will shatter chiefs
      over the wide earth.

7 He will drink from the brook by the way;
      therefore he will lift up his head.

OCTOBER 8
~ Psalm 111

Great Are the Lord's *Works*

1 Praise the Lord!
I will give thanks to the Lord with my whole heart,
 in the company of the upright, in the congregation.
2 Great are the works of the Lord,
 studied by all who delight in them.
3 Full of splendor and majesty is his work,
 and his righteousness endures forever.
4 He has caused his wondrous works to be remembered;
 the Lord is gracious and merciful.
5 He provides food for those who fear him;
 he remembers his covenant forever.
6 He has shown his people the power of his works,
 in giving them the inheritance of the nations.
7 The works of his hands are faithful and just;
 all his precepts are trustworthy;
8 they are established forever and ever,
 to be performed with faithfulness and uprightness.
9 He sent redemption to his people;
 he has commanded his covenant forever.
 Holy and awesome is his name!
10 The fear of the Lord is the beginning of wisdom;
 all those who practice it have a good understanding.
 His praise endures forever!

Reflection

Full of *splendor and majesty* is his work, and his *righteousness* endures forever.

Psalm 111:3

OCTOBER 9
~ Psalm 112

The Righteous Will Never Be Moved

1 Praise the LORD!
Blessed is the man who fears the LORD,
  who greatly delights in his commandments!
2 His offspring will be mighty in the land;
  the generation of the upright will be blessed.
3 Wealth and riches are in his house,
  and his righteousness endures forever.
4 Light dawns in the darkness for the upright;
  he is gracious, merciful, and righteous.
5 It is well with the man who deals generously and lends;
  who conducts his affairs with justice.
6 For the righteous will never be moved;
  he will be remembered forever.
7 He is not afraid of bad news;
  his heart is firm, trusting in the LORD.
8 His heart is steady; he will not be afraid,
  until he looks in triumph on his adversaries.
9 He has distributed freely; he has given to the poor;
  his righteousness endures forever;
  his horn is exalted in honor.
10 The wicked man sees it and is angry;
  he gnashes his teeth and melts away;
  the desire of the wicked will perish!

Reflection

OCTOBER 10
~ Psalm 113

Who Is like the *Lord Our God?*

1 Praise the LORD!
Praise, O servants of the LORD,
    praise the name of the LORD!

2 Blessed be the name of the LORD
    from this time forth and forevermore!
3 From the rising of the sun to its setting,
    the name of the LORD is to be praised!

4 The LORD is high above all nations,
    and his glory above the heavens!
5 Who is like the LORD our God,
    who is seated on high,
6 who looks far down
    on the heavens and the earth?
7 He raises the poor from the dust
    and lifts the needy from the ash heap,
8 to make them sit with princes,
    with the princes of his people.
9 He gives the barren woman a home,
    making her the joyous mother of children.
Praise the LORD!

Reflection

OCTOBER 11
~ Psalm 114

Tremble at the *Presence of the Lord*

1   When Israel went out from Egypt,
     the house of Jacob from a people of strange language,
2   Judah became his sanctuary,
     Israel his dominion.

3   The sea looked and fled;
     Jordan turned back.
4   The mountains skipped like rams,
     the hills like lambs.

5   What ails you, O sea, that you flee?
     O Jordan, that you turn back?
6   O mountains, that you skip like rams?
     O hills, like lambs?

7   Tremble, O earth, at the presence of the Lord,
     at the presence of the God of Jacob,
8   who turns the rock into a pool of water,
     the flint into a spring of water.

Reflection

OCTOBER 12
~ Psalm 115:1-6

To Your Name Give Glory

1 Not to us, O LORD, not to us, but to your name give glory,
    for the sake of your steadfast love and your faithfulness!

2 Why should the nations say,
    "Where is their God?"

3 Our God is in the heavens;
    he does all that he pleases.

4 Their idols are silver and gold,
    the work of human hands.

5 They have mouths, but do not speak;
    eyes, but do not see.

6 They have ears, but do not hear;
    noses, but do not smell.

Reflection

OCTOBER 13
~ Psalm 115:7-11

7   They have hands, but do not feel;
      feet, but do not walk;
      and they do not make a sound in their throat.
8   Those who make them become like them;
      so do all who trust in them.

9   O Israel, trust in the LORD!
      He is their help and their shield.
10   O house of Aaron, trust in the LORD!
      He is their help and their shield.
11   You who fear the LORD, trust in the LORD!
      He is their help and their shield.

Reflection

OCTOBER 14
~ Psalm 115:12-18

12   The LORD has remembered us; he will bless us;
         he will bless the house of Israel;
         he will bless the house of Aaron;
13   he will bless those who fear the LORD,
         both the small and the great.

14   May the LORD give you increase,
         you and your children!
15   May you be blessed by the LORD,
         who made heaven and earth!

16   The heavens are the LORD's heavens,
         but the earth he has given to the children of man.
17   The dead do not praise the LORD,
         nor do any who go down into silence.
18   But we will bless the LORD
         from this time forth and forevermore.
         Praise the LORD!

Reflection

OCTOBER 15
~ Psalm 116:1-9

I Love the LORD

1   I love the LORD, because he has heard
        my voice and my pleas for mercy.
2   Because he inclined his ear to me,
        therefore I will call on him as long as I live.
3   The snares of death encompassed me;
        the pangs of Sheol laid hold on me;
        I suffered distress and anguish.
4   Then I called on the name of the LORD:
        "O LORD, I pray, deliver my soul!"

5   Gracious is the LORD, and righteous;
        our God is merciful.
6   The LORD preserves the simple;
        when I was brought low, he saved me.
7   Return, O my soul, to your rest;
        for the LORD has dealt bountifully with you.

8   For you have delivered my soul from death,
        my eyes from tears,
        my feet from stumbling;
9   I will walk before the LORD
        in the land of the living.

Reflection

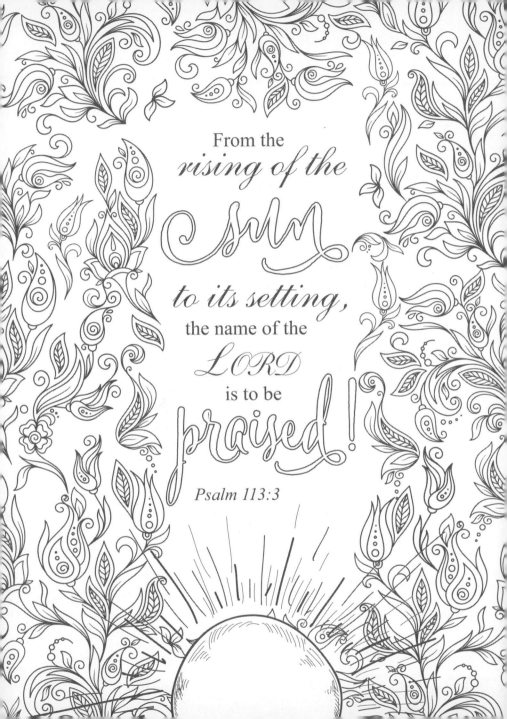

From the
rising of the

sun

to its setting,
the name of the

LORD
is to be

praised!

Psalm 113:3

OCTOBER 16

10   I believed, even when I spoke:
          " I am greatly afflicted";
11   I said in my alarm,
          " All mankind are liars."

12   What shall I render to the LORD
          for all his benefits to me?
13   I will lift up the cup of salvation
          and call on the name of the LORD,
14   I will pay my vows to the LORD
          in the presence of all his people.

15   Precious in the sight of the LORD
          is the death of his saints.
16   O LORD, I am your servant;
          I am your servant, the son of your maidservant.
          You have loosed my bonds.
17   I will offer to you the sacrifice of thanksgiving
          and call on the name of the LORD.
18   I will pay my vows to the LORD
          in the presence of all his people,
19   in the courts of the house of the LORD,
          in your midst, O Jerusalem.
          Praise the LORD!

Reflection

OCTOBER 17
~ Psalm 117

The LORD's *Faithfulness* Endures Forever

1   Praise the LORD, all nations!
       Extol him, all peoples!
2   For great is his steadfast love toward us,
       and the faithfulness of the LORD endures forever.
   Praise the LORD!

Reflection

OCTOBER 18
~ Psalm 118:1-7

His Steadfast Love Endures Forever

1 Oh give thanks to the LORD, for he is good;
   for his steadfast love endures forever!

2 Let Israel say,
   " His steadfast love endures forever."
3 Let the house of Aaron say,
   " His steadfast love endures forever."
4 Let those who fear the LORD say,
   " His steadfast love endures forever."

5 Out of my distress I called on the LORD;
   the LORD answered me and set me free.
6 The LORD is on my side; I will not fear.
   What can man do to me?
7 The LORD is on my side as my helper;
   I shall look in triumph on those who hate me.

Reflection

_____

_____

_____

_____

_____

_____

_____

_____

_____

OCTOBER 19
~ Psalm 118:8-16

8   It is better to take refuge in the LORD
       than to trust in man.

9   It is better to take refuge in the LORD
       than to trust in princes.

10   All nations surrounded me;
       in the name of the LORD I cut them off!

11   They surrounded me, surrounded me on every side;
       in the name of the LORD I cut them off!

12   They surrounded me like bees;
       they went out like a fire among thorns;
       in the name of the LORD I cut them off!

13   I was pushed hard, so that I was falling,
       but the LORD helped me.

14   The LORD is my strength and my song;
       he has become my salvation.

15   Glad songs of salvation
       are in the tents of the righteous:
   "The right hand of the LORD does valiantly,

16   the right hand of the LORD exalts,
       the right hand of the LORD does valiantly!"

Reflection

OCTOBER 20
~ Psalm 118:17-24

17   I shall not die, but I shall live,
       and recount the deeds of the LORD.

18   The LORD has disciplined me severely,
       but he has not given me over to death.

19   Open to me the gates of righteousness,
       that I may enter through them
       and give thanks to the LORD.

20   This is the gate of the LORD;
       the righteous shall enter through it.

21   I thank you that you have answered me
       and have become my salvation.

22   The stone that the builders rejected
       has become the cornerstone.

23   This is the LORD's doing;
       it is marvelous in our eyes.

24   This is the day that the LORD has made;
       let us rejoice and be glad in it.

Reflection

OCTOBER 21
~ Psalm 118:25-29

25   Save us, we pray, O LORD!
        O LORD, we pray, give us success!

26   Blessed is he who comes in the name of the LORD!
        We bless you from the house of the LORD.

27   The LORD is God,
        and he has made his light to shine upon us.
    Bind the festal sacrifice with cords,
        up to the horns of the altar!

28   You are my God, and I will give thanks to you;
        you are my God; I will extol you.

29   Oh give thanks to the LORD, for he is good;
        for his steadfast love endures forever!

Reflection

OCTOBER 22
~ Psalm 119:1-8

Your Word Is a Lamp to My Feet

ALEPH

1   Blessed are those whose way is blameless,
       who walk in the law of the LORD!
2   Blessed are those who keep his testimonies,
       who seek him with their whole heart,
3   who also do no wrong,
       but walk in his ways!
4   You have commanded your precepts
       to be kept diligently.
5   Oh that my ways may be steadfast
       in keeping your statutes!
6   Then I shall not be put to shame,
       having my eyes fixed on all your commandments.
7   I will praise you with an upright heart,
       when I learn your righteous rules.
8   I will keep your statutes;
       do not utterly forsake me!

Reflection

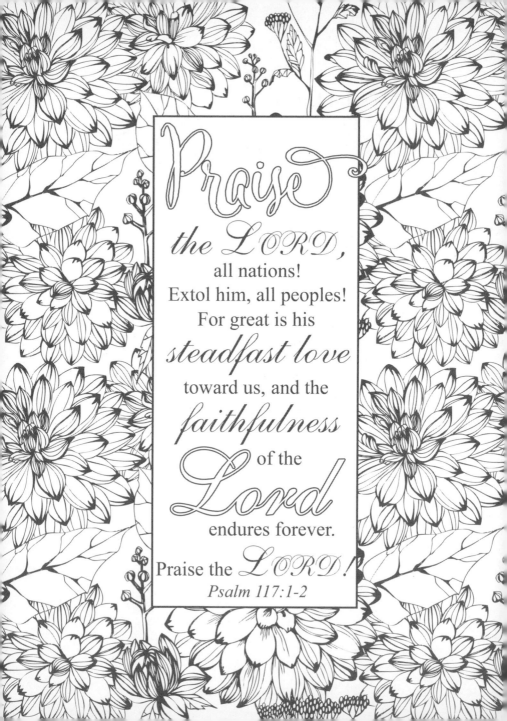

Praise the LORD, all nations! Extol him, all peoples! For great is his steadfast love toward us, and the faithfulness of the Lord endures forever. Praise the LORD!

Psalm 117:1-2

OCTOBER 23
~ Psalm 119:9-16

BETH

9 How can a young man keep his way pure?
   By guarding it according to your word.
10 With my whole heart I seek you;
   let me not wander from your commandments!
11 I have stored up your word in my heart,
   that I might not sin against you.
12 Blessed are you, O LORD;
   teach me your statutes!
13 With my lips I declare
   all the rules of your mouth.
14 In the way of your testimonies I delight
   as much as in all riches.
15 I will meditate on your precepts
   and fix my eyes on your ways.
16 I will delight in your statutes;
   I will not forget your word.

Reflection

OCTOBER 24
~ Psalm 119:17-24

GIMEL

17 Deal bountifully with your servant,
   that I may live and keep your word.
18 Open my eyes, that I may behold
   wondrous things out of your law.
19 I am a sojourner on the earth;
   hide not your commandments from me!
20 My soul is consumed with longing
   for your rules at all times.
21 You rebuke the insolent, accursed ones,
   who wander from your commandments.
22 Take away from me scorn and contempt,
   for I have kept your testimonies.
23 Even though princes sit plotting against me,
   your servant will meditate on your statutes.
24 Your testimonies are my delight;
   they are my counselors.

Reflection

OCTOBER 25
~ Psalm 119:25-32

DALETH

25   My soul clings to the dust;
    give me life according to your word!
26   When I told of my ways, you answered me;
    teach me your statutes!
27   Make me understand the way of your precepts,
    and I will meditate on your wondrous works.
28   My soul melts away for sorrow;
    strengthen me according to your word!
29   Put false ways far from me
    and graciously teach me your law!
30   I have chosen the way of faithfulness;
    I set your rules before me.
31   I cling to your testimonies, O LORD;
    let me not be put to shame!
32   I will run in the way of your commandments
    when you enlarge my heart!

Reflection

OCTOBER 26
~ Psalm 119:33-40

H E

33 Teach me, O LORD, the way of your statutes;
    and I will keep it to the end.

34 Give me understanding, that I may keep your law
    and observe it with my whole heart.

35 Lead me in the path of your commandments,
    for I delight in it.

36 Incline my heart to your testimonies,
    and not to selfish gain!

37 Turn my eyes from looking at worthless things;
    and give me life in your ways.

38 Confirm to your servant your promise,
    that you may be feared.

39 Turn away the reproach that I dread,
    for your rules are good.

40 Behold, I long for your precepts;
    in your righteousness give me life!

Reflection

OCTOBER 27
~ Psalm 119:41-48

WAW

41 Let your steadfast love come to me, O LORD,
   your salvation according to your promise;
42 then shall I have an answer for him who taunts me,
   for I trust in your word.
43 And take not the word of truth utterly out of my mouth,
   for my hope is in your rules.
44 I will keep your law continually,
   forever and ever,
45 and I shall walk in a wide place,
   for I have sought your precepts.
46 I will also speak of your testimonies before kings
   and shall not be put to shame,
47 for I find my delight in your commandments,
   which I love.
48 I will lift up my hands toward your commandments,
   which I love,
   and I will meditate on your statutes.

Reflection

OCTOBER 28
~ Psalm 119:49-56

49 Remember your word to your servant,
   in which you have made me hope.
50 This is my comfort in my affliction,
   that your promise gives me life.
51 The insolent utterly deride me,
   but I do not turn away from your law.
52 When I think of your rules from of old,
   I take comfort, O LORD.
53 Hot indignation seizes me because of the wicked,
   who forsake your law.
54 Your statutes have been my songs
   in the house of my sojourning.
55 I remember your name in the night, O LORD,
   and keep your law.
56 This blessing has fallen to me,
   that I have kept your precepts.

Reflection

OCTOBER 29
~ Psalm 119:57-64

HETH

57   The LORD is my portion;
         I promise to keep your words.
58   I entreat your favor with all my heart;
         be gracious to me according to your promise.
59   When I think on my ways,
         I turn my feet to your testimonies;
60   I hasten and do not delay
         to keep your commandments.
61   Though the cords of the wicked ensnare me,
         I do not forget your law.
62   At midnight I rise to praise you,
         because of your righteous rules.
63   I am a companion of all who fear you,
         of those who keep your precepts.
64   The earth, O LORD, is full of your steadfast love;
         teach me your statutes!

Reflection

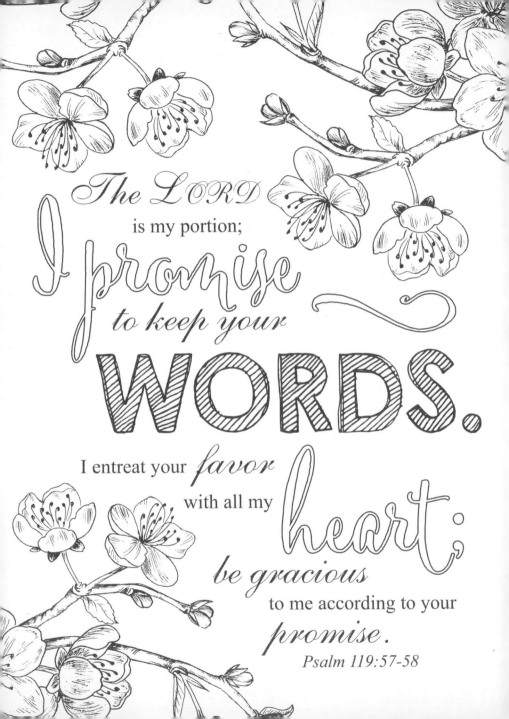

The LORD is my portion; I promise to keep your WORDS. I entreat your favor with all my heart; be gracious to me according to your promise.

Psalm 119:57-58

OCTOBER 30
~ Psalm 119:65-72

TETH

65 You have dealt well with your servant,
    O LORD, according to your word.
66 Teach me good judgment and knowledge,
    for I believe in your commandments.
67 Before I was afflicted I went astray,
    but now I keep your word.
68 You are good and do good;
    teach me your statutes.
69 The insolent smear me with lies,
    but with my whole heart I keep your precepts;
70 their heart is unfeeling like fat,
    but I delight in your law.
71 It is good for me that I was afflicted,
    that I might learn your statutes.
72 The law of your mouth is better to me
    than thousands of gold and silver pieces.

Reflection

OCTOBER 31
~ Psalm 119:73-80

YODH

73 Your hands have made and fashioned me;
  give me understanding that I may learn your
    commandments.

74 Those who fear you shall see me and rejoice,
  because I have hoped in your word.

75 I know, O LORD, that your rules are righteous,
  and that in faithfulness you have afflicted me.

76 Let your steadfast love comfort me
  according to your promise to your servant.

77 Let your mercy come to me, that I may live;
  for your law is my delight.

78 Let the insolent be put to shame,
  because they have wronged me with falsehood;
  as for me, I will meditate on your precepts.

79 Let those who fear you turn to me,
  that they may know your testimonies.

80 May my heart be blameless in your statutes,
  that I may not be put to shame!

Reflection

NOVEMBER 1
~ Psalm 119:81-88

81   My soul longs for your salvation;
      I hope in your word.

82   My eyes long for your promise;
      I ask, "When will you comfort me?"

83   For I have become like a wineskin in the smoke,
      yet I have not forgotten your statutes.

84   How long must your servant endure?
      When will you judge those who persecute me?

85   The insolent have dug pitfalls for me;
      they do not live according to your law.

86   All your commandments are sure;
      they persecute me with falsehood; help me!

87   They have almost made an end of me on earth,
      but I have not forsaken your precepts.

88   In your steadfast love give me life,
      that I may keep the testimonies of your mouth.

Reflection

NOVEMBER 2
~ Psalm 119:89-96

LAMEDH

89 Forever, O LORD, your word
   is firmly fixed in the heavens.
90 Your faithfulness endures to all generations;
   you have established the earth, and it stands fast.
91 By your appointment they stand this day,
   for all things are your servants.
92 If your law had not been my delight,
   I would have perished in my affliction.
93 I will never forget your precepts,
   for by them you have given me life.
94 I am yours; save me,
   for I have sought your precepts.
95 The wicked lie in wait to destroy me,
   but I consider your testimonies.
96 I have seen a limit to all perfection,
   but your commandment is exceedingly broad.

Reflection

NOVEMBER 3
~ Psalm 119:97-104

97   Oh how I love your law!
     It is my meditation all the day.

98   Your commandment makes me wiser than my enemies,
     for it is ever with me.

99   I have more understanding than all my teachers,
     for your testimonies are my meditation.

100   I understand more than the aged,
     for I keep your precepts.

101   I hold back my feet from every evil way,
     in order to keep your word.

102   I do not turn aside from your rules,
     for you have taught me.

103   How sweet are your words to my taste,
     sweeter than honey to my mouth!

104   Through your precepts I get understanding;
     therefore I hate every false way.

Reflection

NOVEMBER 4
~ Psalm 119:105-112

NUN

105   Your word is a lamp to my feet
    and a light to my path.

106   I have sworn an oath and confirmed it,
    to keep your righteous rules.

107   I am severely afflicted;
    give me life, O LORD, according to your word!

108   Accept my freewill offerings of praise, O LORD,
    and teach me your rules.

109   I hold my life in my hand continually,
    but I do not forget your law.

110   The wicked have laid a snare for me,
    but I do not stray from your precepts.

111   Your testimonies are my heritage forever,
    for they are the joy of my heart.

112   I incline my heart to perform your statutes
    forever, to the end.

Reflection

NOVEMBER 5
~ Psalm 119:113-120

SAMEKH

113 I hate the double-minded,
   but I love your law.
114 You are my hiding place and my shield;
   I hope in your word.
115 Depart from me, you evildoers,
   that I may keep the commandments of my God.
116 Uphold me according to your promise, that I may live,
   and let me not be put to shame in my hope!
117 Hold me up, that I may be safe
   and have regard for your statutes continually!
118 You spurn all who go astray from your statutes,
   for their cunning is in vain.
119 All the wicked of the earth you discard like dross,
   therefore I love your testimonies.
120 My flesh trembles for fear of you,
   and I am afraid of your judgments.

Reflection

Your word is a lamp to my feet and a light to my path.

Psalm 119:105

NOVEMBER 6
~ Psalm 119:121-128

121 I have done what is just and right;
   do not leave me to my oppressors.

122 Give your servant a pledge of good;
   let not the insolent oppress me.

123 My eyes long for your salvation
   and for the fulfillment of your righteous promise.

124 Deal with your servant according to your steadfast love,
   and teach me your statutes.

125 I am your servant; give me understanding,
   that I may know your testimonies!

126 It is time for the LORD to act,
   for your law has been broken.

127 Therefore I love your commandments
   above gold, above fine gold.

128 Therefore I consider all your precepts to be right;
   I hate every false way.

Reflection

NOVEMBER 7
~ Psalm 119:129-136

PE

129 Your testimonies are wonderful;
therefore my soul keeps them.
130 The unfolding of your words gives light;
it imparts understanding to the simple.
131 I open my mouth and pant,
because I long for your commandments.
132 Turn to me and be gracious to me,
as is your way with those who love your name.
133 Keep steady my steps according to your promise,
and let no iniquity get dominion over me.
134 Redeem me from man's oppression,
that I may keep your precepts.
135 Make your face shine upon your servant,
and teach me your statutes.
136 My eyes shed streams of tears,
because people do not keep your law.

Reflection

NOVEMBER 8
~ Psalm 119:137-144

137 Righteous are you, O LORD,
   and right are your rules.

138 You have appointed your testimonies in righteousness
   and in all faithfulness.

139 My zeal consumes me,
   because my foes forget your words.

140 Your promise is well tried,
   and your servant loves it.

141 I am small and despised,
   yet I do not forget your precepts.

142 Your righteousness is righteous forever,
   and your law is true.

143 Trouble and anguish have found me out,
   but your commandments are my delight.

144 Your testimonies are righteous forever;
   give me understanding that I may live.

Reflection

NOVEMBER 9
~ Psalm 119:145-152

QOPH

145   With my whole heart I cry; answer me, O LORD!
      I will keep your statutes.

146   I call to you; save me,
      that I may observe your testimonies.

147   I rise before dawn and cry for help;
      I hope in your words.

148   My eyes are awake before the watches of the night,
      that I may meditate on your promise.

149   Hear my voice according to your steadfast love;
      O LORD, according to your justice give me life.

150   They draw near who persecute me with evil purpose;
      they are far from your law.

151   But you are near, O LORD,
      and all your commandments are true.

152   Long have I known from your testimonies
      that you have founded them forever.

Reflection

NOVEMBER 10
~ Psalm 119:153-160

RESH

153 Look on my affliction and deliver me,
for I do not forget your law.
154 Plead my cause and redeem me;
give me life according to your promise!
155 Salvation is far from the wicked,
for they do not seek your statutes.
156 Great is your mercy, O LORD;
give me life according to your rules.
157 Many are my persecutors and my adversaries,
but I do not swerve from your testimonies.
158 I look at the faithless with disgust,
because they do not keep your commands.
159 Consider how I love your precepts!
Give me life according to your steadfast love.
160 The sum of your word is truth,
and every one of your righteous rules endures forever.

NOVEMBER 11
~ Psalm 119:161-168

161 Princes persecute me without cause,
but my heart stands in awe of your words.

162 I rejoice at your word
like one who finds great spoil.

163 I hate and abhor falsehood,
but I love your law.

164 Seven times a day I praise you
for your righteous rules.

165 Great peace have those who love your law;
nothing can make them stumble.

166 I hope for your salvation, O LORD,
and I do your commandments.

167 My soul keeps your testimonies;
I love them exceedingly.

168 I keep your precepts and testimonies,
for all my ways are before you.

Reflection

NOVEMBER 12
~ Psalm 119:169-176

TAW

169   Let my cry come before you, O LORD;
        give me understanding according to your word!

170   Let my plea come before you;
        deliver me according to your word.

171   My lips will pour forth praise,
        for you teach me your statutes.

172   My tongue will sing of your word,
        for all your commandments are right.

173   Let your hand be ready to help me,
        for I have chosen your precepts.

174   I long for your salvation, O LORD,
        and your law is my delight.

175   Let my soul live and praise you,
        and let your rules help me.

176   I have gone astray like a lost sheep; seek your servant,
        for I do not forget your commandments.

Reflection

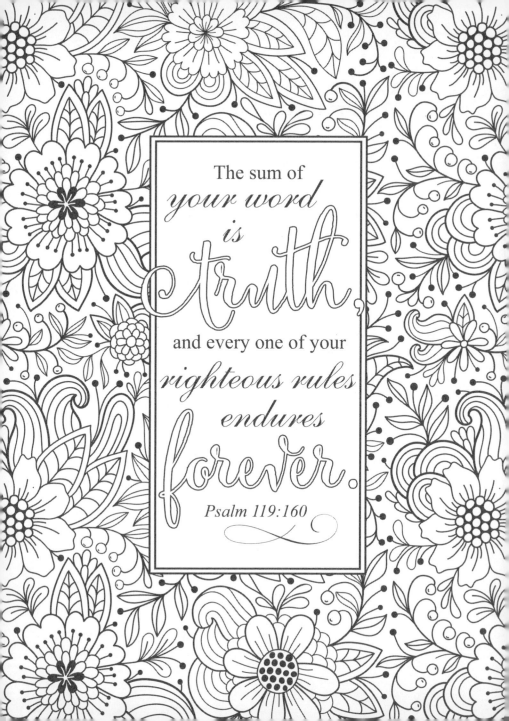

The sum of *your word* *is* truth, and every one of your *righteous rules* *endures* forever.

Psalm 119:160

NOVEMBER 13
~ Psalm 120

Deliver Me, O Lord

A Song of Ascents.

1 In my distress I called to the LORD,
   and he answered me.
2 Deliver me, O LORD,
   from lying lips,
   from a deceitful tongue.

3 What shall be given to you,
   and what more shall be done to you,
   you deceitful tongue?
4 A warrior's sharp arrows,
   with glowing coals of the broom tree!

5 Woe to me, that I sojourn in Meshech,
   that I dwell among the tents of Kedar!
6 Too long have I had my dwelling
   among those who hate peace.
7 I am for peace,
   but when I speak, they are for war!

Reflection

NOVEMBER 14
~ Psalm 121

My Help Comes from *the Lord*

A Song of Ascents.

1 I lift up my eyes to the hills.
    From where does my help come?
2 My help comes from the LORD,
    who made heaven and earth.

3 He will not let your foot be moved;
    he who keeps you will not slumber.
4 Behold, he who keeps Israel
    will neither slumber nor sleep.

5 The LORD is your keeper;
    the LORD is your shade on your right hand.
6 The sun shall not strike you by day,
    nor the moon by night.

7 The LORD will keep you from all evil;
    he will keep your life.
8 The LORD will keep
    your going out and your coming in
    from this time forth and forevermore.

Reflection

NOVEMBER 15
~ Psalm 122

Let Us Go to *the House* of the LORD

A Song of Ascents. Of David.

1 I was glad when they said to me,
   " Let us go to the house of the LORD!"
2 Our feet have been standing
   within your gates, O Jerusalem!

3 Jerusalem—built as a city
   that is bound firmly together,
4 to which the tribes go up,
   the tribes of the LORD,
as was decreed for Israel,
   to give thanks to the name of the LORD.
5 There thrones for judgment were set,
   the thrones of the house of David.

6 Pray for the peace of Jerusalem!
   " May they be secure who love you!
7 Peace be within your walls
   and security within your towers!"
8 For my brothers and companions' sake
   I will say, "Peace be within you!"
9 For the sake of the house of the LORD our God,
   I will seek your good.

Reflection

_____

_____

_____

_____

NOVEMBER 16
~ Psalm 123

Our Eyes Look to the Lord Our God

A Song of Ascents.

1 To you I lift up my eyes,
   O you who are enthroned in the heavens!
2 Behold, as the eyes of servants
   look to the hand of their master,
as the eyes of a maidservant
   to the hand of her mistress,
so our eyes look to the LORD our God,
   till he has mercy upon us.

3 Have mercy upon us, O LORD, have mercy upon us,
   for we have had more than enough of contempt.
4 Our soul has had more than enough
   of the scorn of those who are at ease,
   of the contempt of the proud.

Reflection

_____

_____

_____

_____

_____

_____

~ Psalm 124

Our Help Is in the Name of the LORD

A Song of Ascents. Of David.

1   If it had not been the LORD who was on our side—
     let Israel now say—
2   if it had not been the LORD who was on our side
     when people rose up against us,
3   then they would have swallowed us up alive,
     when their anger was kindled against us;
4   then the flood would have swept us away,
     the torrent would have gone over us;
5   then over us would have gone
     the raging waters.

6   Blessed be the LORD,
     who has not given us
     as prey to their teeth!
7   We have escaped like a bird
     from the snare of the fowlers;
   the snare is broken,
     and we have escaped!

8   Our help is in the name of the LORD,
     who made heaven and earth.

Reflection

NOVEMBER 18
~ Psalm 125

The Lord Surrounds His People

A Song of Ascents.

1 Those who trust in the LORD are like Mount Zion,
   which cannot be moved, but abides forever.
2 As the mountains surround Jerusalem,
   so the LORD surrounds his people,
   from this time forth and forevermore.
3 For the scepter of wickedness shall not rest
   on the land allotted to the righteous,
   lest the righteous stretch out
   their hands to do wrong.
4 Do good, O LORD, to those who are good,
   and to those who are upright in their hearts!
5 But those who turn aside to their crooked ways
   the LORD will lead away with evildoers!
   Peace be upon Israel!

Reflection

NOVEMBER 19
~ Psalm 126

Restore Our Fortunes, O Lord

A Song of Ascents.

1 When the LORD restored the fortunes of Zion,
    we were like those who dream.
2 Then our mouth was filled with laughter,
    and our tongue with shouts of joy;
  then they said among the nations,
    "The LORD has done great things for them."
3 The LORD has done great things for us;
    we are glad.

4 Restore our fortunes, O LORD,
    like streams in the Negeb!
5 Those who sow in tears
    shall reap with shouts of joy!
6 He who goes out weeping,
    bearing the seed for sowing,
  shall come home with shouts of joy,
    bringing his sheaves with him.

Reflection

I lift up my eyes to the hills. From where does my help come? My help comes from the Lord, who made heaven and earth. *Psalm 121:1-2*

NOVEMBER 20
~ Psalm 127

Unless the Lord Builds the House

A Song of Ascents. Of Solomon.

1 Unless the LORD builds the house,
   those who build it labor in vain.
Unless the LORD watches over the city,
   the watchman stays awake in vain.
2 It is in vain that you rise up early
   and go late to rest,
eating the bread of anxious toil;
   for he gives to his beloved sleep.

3 Behold, children are a heritage from the LORD,
   the fruit of the womb a reward.
4 Like arrows in the hand of a warrior
   are the children of one's youth.
5 Blessed is the man
   who fills his quiver with them!
He shall not be put to shame
   when he speaks with his enemies in the gate.

Reflection

NOVEMBER 21
~ Psalm 128

Blessed Is Everyone Who Fears the Lord

A Song of Ascents.

1 Blessed is everyone who fears the LORD,
   who walks in his ways!
2 You shall eat the fruit of the labor of your hands;
   you shall be blessed, and it shall be well with you.

3 Your wife will be like a fruitful vine
   within your house;
 your children will be like olive shoots
   around your table.
4 Behold, thus shall the man be blessed
   who fears the LORD.

5 The LORD bless you from Zion!
   May you see the prosperity of Jerusalem
   all the days of your life!
6 May you see your children's children!
   Peace be upon Israel!

Reflection

NOVEMBER 22

~ Psalm 129

They Have *Afflicted Me* from *My Youth*

A Song of Ascents.

1 " Greatly have they afflicted me from my youth"—
   let Israel now say—
2 " Greatly have they afflicted me from my youth,
   yet they have not prevailed against me.
3 The plowers plowed upon my back;
   they made long their furrows."
4 The LORD is righteous;
   he has cut the cords of the wicked.
5 May all who hate Zion
   be put to shame and turned backward!
6 Let them be like the grass on the housetops,
   which withers before it grows up,
7 with which the reaper does not fill his hand
   nor the binder of sheaves his arms,
8 nor do those who pass by say,
   " The blessing of the LORD be upon you!
   We bless you in the name of the LORD!"

Reflection

NOVEMBER 23
~ Psalm 130

My Soul Waits for *the Lord*

A Song of Ascents.

1 Out of the depths I cry to you, O LORD!
2   O Lord, hear my voice!
    Let your ears be attentive
        to the voice of my pleas for mercy!

3 If you, O LORD, should mark iniquities,
    O Lord, who could stand?
4 But with you there is forgiveness,
    that you may be feared.

5 I wait for the LORD, my soul waits,
    and in his word I hope;
6 my soul waits for the Lord
    more than watchmen for the morning,
    more than watchmen for the morning.

7 O Israel, hope in the LORD!
    For with the LORD there is steadfast love,
    and with him is plentiful redemption.
8 And he will redeem Israel
    from all his iniquities.

Reflection

NOVEMBER 24
~ Psalm 131

I Have Calmed & Quieted My Soul

A Song of Ascents. Of David.

1 O LORD, my heart is not lifted up;
   my eyes are not raised too high;
  I do not occupy myself with things
   too great and too marvelous for me.
2 But I have calmed and quieted my soul,
   like a weaned child with its mother;
   like a weaned child is my soul within me.

3 O Israel, hope in the LORD
   from this time forth and forevermore.

Reflection

NOVEMBER 25
~ Psalm 132:1-7

The Lord Has Chosen Zion

A Song of Ascents.

1 Remember, O LORD, in David's favor,
   all the hardships he endured,
2 how he swore to the LORD
   and vowed to the Mighty One of Jacob,
3 "I will not enter my house
   or get into my bed,
4 I will not give sleep to my eyes
   or slumber to my eyelids,
5 until I find a place for the LORD,
   a dwelling place for the Mighty One of Jacob."

6 Behold, we heard of it in Ephrathah;
   we found it in the fields of Jaar.
7 "Let us go to his dwelling place;
   let us worship at his footstool!"

Reflection

NOVEMBER 26
~ Psalm 132:8-12

8   Arise, O Lord, and go to your resting place,
         you and the ark of your might.
9   Let your priests be clothed with righteousness,
         and let your saints shout for joy.
10   For the sake of your servant David,
         do not turn away the face of your anointed one.

11   The Lord swore to David a sure oath
         from which he will not turn back:
    "One of the sons of your body
         I will set on your throne.
12   If your sons keep my covenant
         and my testimonies that I shall teach them,
    their sons also forever
         shall sit on your throne."

Reflection

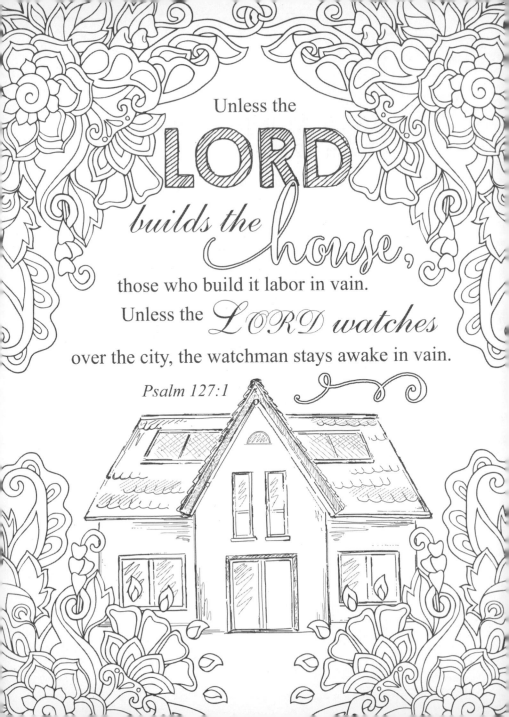

NOVEMBER 27
~ Psalm 132:13-18

13   For the Lord has chosen Zion;
        he has desired it for his dwelling place:

14   "This is my resting place forever;
        here I will dwell, for I have desired it.

15   I will abundantly bless her provisions;
        I will satisfy her poor with bread.

16   Her priests I will clothe with salvation,
        and her saints will shout for joy.

17   There I will make a horn to sprout for David;
        I have prepared a lamp for my anointed.

18   His enemies I will clothe with shame,
        but on him his crown will shine."

Reflection

NOVEMBER 28
~ Psalm 133

When Brothers Dwell in Unity

A Song of Ascents. Of David.

1   Behold, how good and pleasant it is
        when brothers dwell in unity!
2   It is like the precious oil on the head,
        running down on the beard,
    on the beard of Aaron,
        running down on the collar of his robes!
3   It is like the dew of Hermon,
        which falls on the mountains of Zion!
    For there the LORD has commanded the blessing,
        life forevermore.

Reflection

NOVEMBER 29
~ Psalm 134

Come, *Bless the Lord* ✌

A Song of Ascents.

1   Come, bless the LORD, all you servants of the LORD,
    who stand by night in the house of the LORD!
2   Lift up your hands to the holy place
    and bless the LORD!

3   May the LORD bless you from Zion,
    he who made heaven and earth!

Reflection

_____

_____

_____

_____

_____

_____

_____

_____

_____

_____

_____

NOVEMBER 30
~ Psalm 135:1-7

Your Name, O Lord, Endures Forever

1 Praise the LORD!
 Praise the name of the LORD,
 give praise, O servants of the LORD,
2 who stand in the house of the LORD,
 in the courts of the house of our God!
3 Praise the LORD, for the LORD is good;
 sing to his name, for it is pleasant!
4 For the LORD has chosen Jacob for himself,
 Israel as his own possession.

5 For I know that the LORD is great,
 and that our Lord is above all gods.
6 Whatever the LORD pleases, he does,
 in heaven and on earth,
 in the seas and all deeps.
7 He it is who makes the clouds rise at the end of the earth,
 who makes lightnings for the rain
 and brings forth the wind from his storehouses.

Reflection

DECEMBER 1
~ Psalm 135:8-14

8   He it was who struck down the firstborn of Egypt,
        both of man and of beast;
9   who in your midst, O Egypt,
        sent signs and wonders
        against Pharaoh and all his servants;
10   who struck down many nations
        and killed mighty kings,
11   Sihon, king of the Amorites,
        and Og, king of Bashan,
        and all the kingdoms of Canaan,
12   and gave their land as a heritage,
        a heritage to his people Israel.

13   Your name, O LORD, endures forever,
        your renown, O LORD, throughout all ages.
14   For the LORD will vindicate his people
        and have compassion on his servants.

Reflection

DECEMBER 2
~ Psalm 135:15-21

15   The idols of the nations are silver and gold,
       the work of human hands.
16   They have mouths, but do not speak;
       they have eyes, but do not see;
17   they have ears, but do not hear,
       nor is there any breath in their mouths.
18   Those who make them become like them,
       so do all who trust in them.

19   O house of Israel, bless the LORD!
       O house of Aaron, bless the LORD!
20   O house of Levi, bless the LORD!
       You who fear the LORD, bless the LORD!
21   Blessed be the LORD from Zion,
       he who dwells in Jerusalem!
       Praise the LORD!

Reflection

DECEMBER 3
~ Psalm 136:1-6

His Steadfast Love Endures Forever

1 Give thanks to the LORD, for he is good,
   for his steadfast love endures forever.
2 Give thanks to the God of gods,
   for his steadfast love endures forever.
3 Give thanks to the Lord of lords,
   for his steadfast love endures forever;

4 to him who alone does great wonders,
   for his steadfast love endures forever;
5 to him who by understanding made the heavens,
   for his steadfast love endures forever;
6 to him who spread out the earth above the waters,
   for his steadfast love endures forever;

Reflection

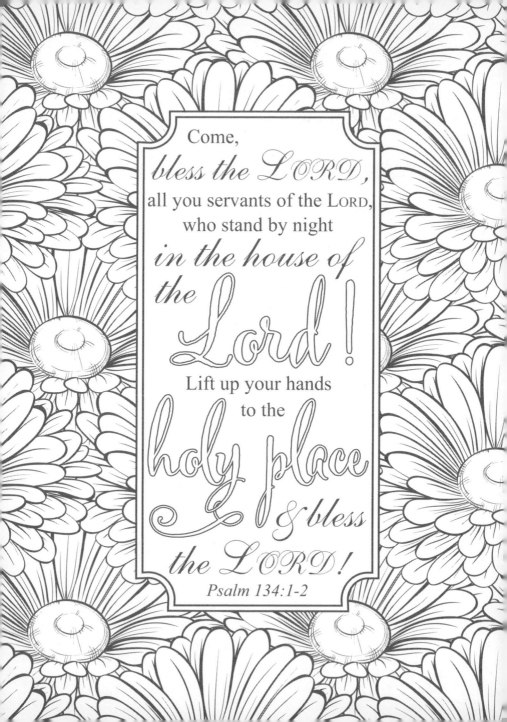

Come,
bless the LORD,
all you servants of the LORD,
who stand by night
in the house of
the
Lord!
Lift up your hands
to the
holy place
& bless
the LORD!
Psalm 134:1-2

DECEMBER 4
~ Psalm 136:7-12

7   to him who made the great lights,
        for his steadfast love endures forever;
8   the sun to rule over the day,
        for his steadfast love endures forever;
9   the moon and stars to rule over the night,
        for his steadfast love endures forever;

10   to him who struck down the firstborn of Egypt,
        for his steadfast love endures forever;
11   and brought Israel out from among them,
        for his steadfast love endures forever;
12   with a strong hand and an outstretched arm,
        for his steadfast love endures forever;

Reflection

DECEMBER 5
~ Psalm 136:13-18

13   to him who divided the Red Sea in two,
        for his steadfast love endures forever;

14   and made Israel pass through the midst of it,
        for his steadfast love endures forever;

15   but overthrew Pharaoh and his host in the Red Sea,
        for his steadfast love endures forever;

16   to him who led his people through the wilderness,
        for his steadfast love endures forever;

17   to him who struck down great kings,
        for his steadfast love endures forever;

18   and killed mighty kings,
        for his steadfast love endures forever;

Reflection

DECEMBER 6
~ Psalm 136:19-26

19 Sihon, king of the Amorites,
      for his steadfast love endures forever;
20 and Og, king of Bashan,
      for his steadfast love endures forever;
21 and gave their land as a heritage,
      for his steadfast love endures forever;
22 a heritage to Israel his servant,
      for his steadfast love endures forever.

23 It is he who remembered us in our low estate,
      for his steadfast love endures forever;
24 and rescued us from our foes,
      for his steadfast love endures forever;
25 he who gives food to all flesh,
      for his steadfast love endures forever.

26 Give thanks to the God of heaven,
      for his steadfast love endures forever.

Reflection

DECEMBER 7
~ Psalm 137

How Shall We *Sing the Lord's Song?*

1 By the waters of Babylon,
there we sat down and wept,
when we remembered Zion.
2 On the willows there
we hung up our lyres.
3 For there our captors
required of us songs,
and our tormentors, mirth, saying,
"Sing us one of the songs of Zion!"

4 How shall we sing the LORD's song
in a foreign land?
5 If I forget you, O Jerusalem,
let my right hand forget its skill!
6 Let my tongue stick to the roof of my mouth,
if I do not remember you,
if I do not set Jerusalem
above my highest joy!

7 Remember, O LORD, against the Edomites
the day of Jerusalem,
how they said, "Lay it bare, lay it bare,
down to its foundations!"
8 O daughter of Babylon, doomed to be destroyed,
blessed shall he be who repays you
with what you have done to us!
9 Blessed shall he be who takes your little ones
and dashes them against the rock!

DECEMBER 8
~ Psalm 138

Give Thanks to the Lord

Of David.

1 I give you thanks, O LORD, with my whole heart;
   before the gods I sing your praise;
2 I bow down toward your holy temple
     and give thanks to your name for your steadfast love and
        your faithfulness,
     for you have exalted above all things
     your name and your word.
3 On the day I called, you answered me;
   my strength of soul you increased.

4 All the kings of the earth shall give you thanks, O LORD,
   for they have heard the words of your mouth,
5 and they shall sing of the ways of the LORD,
   for great is the glory of the LORD.
6 For though the LORD is high, he regards the lowly,
   but the haughty he knows from afar.

7 Though I walk in the midst of trouble,
     you preserve my life;
   you stretch out your hand against the wrath of my enemies,
     and your right hand delivers me.
8 The LORD will fulfill his purpose for me;
   your steadfast love, O LORD, endures forever.
   Do not forsake the work of your hands.

Reflection

DECEMBER 9
~ Psalm 139:1-8

Search Me, *O God,* and Know *My Heart*

To the choirmaster. A Psalm of David.

1 O LORD, you have searched me and known me!
2 You know when I sit down and when I rise up;
   you discern my thoughts from afar.
3 You search out my path and my lying down
   and are acquainted with all my ways.
4 Even before a word is on my tongue,
   behold, O LORD, you know it altogether.
5 You hem me in, behind and before,
   and lay your hand upon me.
6 Such knowledge is too wonderful for me;
   it is high; I cannot attain it.

7 Where shall I go from your Spirit?
   Or where shall I flee from your presence?
8 If I ascend to heaven, you are there!
   If I make my bed in Sheol, you are there!

Reflection

DECEMBER 10
~ Psalm 139:9-16

9 If I take the wings of the morning
   and dwell in the uttermost parts of the sea,
10 even there your hand shall lead me,
   and your right hand shall hold me.
11 If I say, "Surely the darkness shall cover me,
   and the light about me be night,"
12 even the darkness is not dark to you;
   the night is bright as the day,
   for darkness is as light with you.

13 For you formed my inward parts;
   you knitted me together in my mother's womb.
14 I praise you, for I am fearfully and wonderfully made.
   Wonderful are your works;
   my soul knows it very well.
15 My frame was not hidden from you,
   when I was being made in secret,
   intricately woven in the depths of the earth.
16 Your eyes saw my unformed substance;
   in your book were written, every one of them,
   the days that were formed for me,
   when as yet there was none of them.

Reflection

The LORD will fulfill his purpose for me; your steadfast love, O LORD, endures forever. Do not forsake the work of your hands.

Psalm 138:8

DECEMBER 11
~ Psalm 139:17-24

17 How precious to me are your thoughts, O God!
    How vast is the sum of them!
18 If I would count them, they are more than the sand.
    I awake, and I am still with you.

19 Oh that you would slay the wicked, O God!
    O men of blood, depart from me!
20 They speak against you with malicious intent;
    your enemies take your name in vain.
21 Do I not hate those who hate you, O LORD?
    And do I not loathe those who rise up against you?
22 I hate them with complete hatred;
    I count them my enemies.

23 Search me, O God, and know my heart!
    Try me and know my thoughts!
24 And see if there be any grievous way in me,
    and lead me in the way everlasting!

Reflection

DECEMBER 12
~ Psalm 140:1-5

Deliver Me, O Lord, from Evil Men

To the choirmaster. A Psalm of David.

1 Deliver me, O LORD, from evil men;
　　preserve me from violent men,
2 who plan evil things in their heart
　　and stir up wars continually.
3 They make their tongue sharp as a serpent's,
　　and under their lips is the venom of asps.　　　　*Selah*

4 Guard me, O LORD, from the hands of the wicked;
　　preserve me from violent men,
　　who have planned to trip up my feet.
5 The arrogant have hidden a trap for me,
　　and with cords they have spread a net;
　　beside the way they have set snares for me.　　　　*Selah*

Reflection

_____
_____
_____
_____
_____
_____
_____
_____
_____
_____

DECEMBER 13
~ Psalm 140:6-13

6   I say to the L ORD, You are my God;
     give ear to the voice of my pleas for mercy, O L ORD!
7   O L ORD, my Lord, the strength of my salvation,
     you have covered my head in the day of battle.
8   Grant not, O L ORD, the desires of the wicked;
     do not further their evil plot, or they will be exalted! *Selah*

9   As for the head of those who surround me,
     let the mischief of their lips overwhelm them!
10   Let burning coals fall upon them!
     Let them be cast into fire,
     into miry pits, no more to rise!
11   Let not the slanderer be established in the land;
     let evil hunt down the violent man speedily!

12   I know that the L ORD will maintain the cause of the afflicted,
     and will execute justice for the needy.
13   Surely the righteous shall give thanks to your name;
     the upright shall dwell in your presence.

Reflection

DECEMBER 14
~ Psalm 141:1-5

Give Ear to My Voice

A Psalm of David.

1   O Lord, I call upon you; hasten to me!
    Give ear to my voice when I call to you!
2   Let my prayer be counted as incense before you,
    and the lifting up of my hands as the evening sacrifice!

3   Set a guard, O Lord, over my mouth;
    keep watch over the door of my lips!
4   Do not let my heart incline to any evil,
    to busy myself with wicked deeds
in company with men who work iniquity,
    and let me not eat of their delicacies!

5   Let a righteous man strike me—it is a kindness;
    let him rebuke me—it is oil for my head;
    let my head not refuse it.
Yet my prayer is continually against their evil deeds.

Reflection

DECEMBER 15
~ Psalm 141:6-10

6   When their judges are thrown over the cliff,
       then they shall hear my words, for they are pleasant.
7   As when one plows and breaks up the earth,
       so shall our bones be scattered at the mouth of Sheol.

8   But my eyes are toward you, O GOD, my Lord;
       in you I seek refuge; leave me not defenseless!
9   Keep me from the trap that they have laid for me
       and from the snares of evildoers!
10   Let the wicked fall into their own nets,
       while I pass by safely.

Reflection

DECEMBER 16
~ Psalm 142

You Are My Refuge

A Maskil of David, when he was in the cave. A Prayer.

1 With my voice I cry out to the LORD;
   with my voice I plead for mercy to the LORD.
2 I pour out my complaint before him;
   I tell my trouble before him.

3 When my spirit faints within me,
   you know my way!
In the path where I walk
   they have hidden a trap for me.
4 Look to the right and see:
   there is none who takes notice of me;
no refuge remains to me;
   no one cares for my soul.

5 I cry to you, O LORD;
   I say, "You are my refuge,
   my portion in the land of the living."
6 Attend to my cry,
   for I am brought very low!
Deliver me from my persecutors,
   for they are too strong for me!
7 Bring me out of prison,
   that I may give thanks to your name!
The righteous will surround me,
   for you will deal bountifully with me.

Reflection

DECEMBER 17
~ Psalm 143:1-6

My Soul Thirsts for *You*

A Psalm of David.

1 Hear my prayer, O LORD;
   give ear to my pleas for mercy!
   In your faithfulness answer me, in your righteousness!
2 Enter not into judgment with your servant,
   for no one living is righteous before you.

3 For the enemy has pursued my soul;
   he has crushed my life to the ground;
   he has made me sit in darkness like those long dead.
4 Therefore my spirit faints within me;
   my heart within me is appalled.

5 I remember the days of old;
   I meditate on all that you have done;
   I ponder the work of your hands.
6 I stretch out my hands to you;
   my soul thirsts for you like a parched land.   *Selah*

Reflection

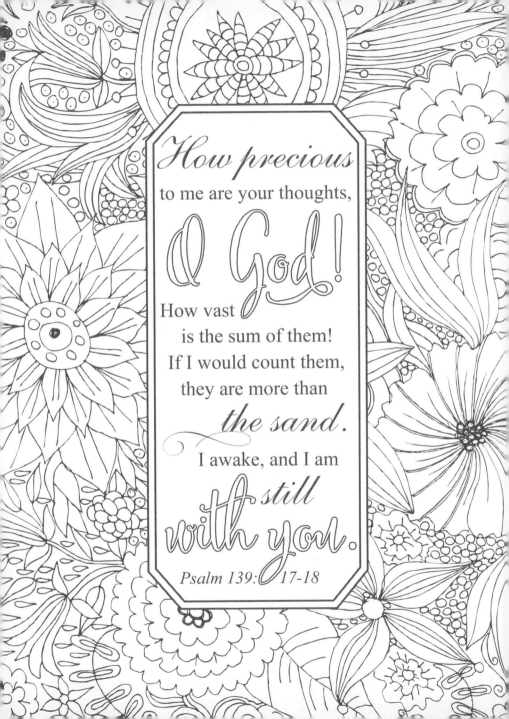

DECEMBER 18
~ Psalm 143:7-12

7   Answer me quickly, O Lord!
      My spirit fails!
    Hide not your face from me,
      lest I be like those who go down to the pit.
8   Let me hear in the morning of your steadfast love,
      for in you I trust.
    Make me know the way I should go,
      for to you I lift up my soul.

9   Deliver me from my enemies, O Lord!
      I have fled to you for refuge.
10 Teach me to do your will,
      for you are my God!
    Let your good Spirit lead me
      on level ground!

11 For your name's sake, O Lord, preserve my life!
      In your righteousness bring my soul out of trouble!
12 And in your steadfast love you will cut off my enemies,
      and you will destroy all the adversaries of my soul,
      for I am your servant.

Reflection

DECEMBER 19
~ Psalm 144:1-8

My Rock and My Fortress

Of David.

1 Blessed be the LORD, my rock,
    who trains my hands for war,
    and my fingers for battle;
2 he is my steadfast love and my fortress,
    my stronghold and my deliverer,
  my shield and he in whom I take refuge,
    who subdues peoples under me.

3 O LORD, what is man that you regard him,
    or the son of man that you think of him?
4 Man is like a breath;
    his days are like a passing shadow.

5 Bow your heavens, O LORD, and come down!
    Touch the mountains so that they smoke!
6 Flash forth the lightning and scatter them;
    send out your arrows and rout them!
7 Stretch out your hand from on high;
    rescue me and deliver me from the many waters,
    from the hand of foreigners,
8 whose mouths speak lies
    and whose right hand is a right hand of falsehood.

Reflection

DECEMBER 20
~ Psalm 144:9-15

[9] I will sing a new song to you, O God;
   upon a ten-stringed harp I will play to you,
[10] who gives victory to kings,
   who rescues David his servant from the cruel sword.
[11] Rescue me and deliver me
   from the hand of foreigners,
whose mouths speak lies
   and whose right hand is a right hand of falsehood.

[12] May our sons in their youth
   be like plants full grown,
our daughters like corner pillars
   cut for the structure of a palace;
[13] may our granaries be full,
   providing all kinds of produce;
may our sheep bring forth thousands
   and ten thousands in our fields;
[14] may our cattle be heavy with young,
   suffering no mishap or failure in bearing;
may there be no cry of distress in our streets!
[15] Blessed are the people to whom such blessings fall!
   Blessed are the people whose God is the Lord!

Reflection

DECEMBER 21
~ Psalm 145:1-7

Great Is the Lord

A Song of Praise. Of David.

1 I will extol you, my God and King,
   and bless your name forever and ever.
2 Every day I will bless you
   and praise your name forever and ever.
3 Great is the LORD, and greatly to be praised,
   and his greatness is unsearchable.

4 One generation shall commend your works to another,
   and shall declare your mighty acts.
5 On the glorious splendor of your majesty,
   and on your wondrous works, I will meditate.
6 They shall speak of the might of your awesome deeds,
   and I will declare your greatness.
7 They shall pour forth the fame of your abundant goodness
   and shall sing aloud of your righteousness.

Reflection

DECEMBER 22
~ Psalm 145:8-14

8   The LORD is gracious and merciful,
        slow to anger and abounding in steadfast love.
9   The LORD is good to all,
        and his mercy is over all that he has made.

10   All your works shall give thanks to you, O LORD,
        and all your saints shall bless you!
11   They shall speak of the glory of your kingdom
        and tell of your power,
12   to make known to the children of man your mighty deeds,
        and the glorious splendor of your kingdom.
13   Your kingdom is an everlasting kingdom,
        and your dominion endures throughout all generations.

     [The LORD is faithful in all his words
        and kind in all his works.]
14   The LORD upholds all who are falling
        and raises up all who are bowed down.

DECEMBER 23
~ Psalm 145:15-21

15   The eyes of all look to you,
           and you give them their food in due season.
16   You open your hand;
           you satisfy the desire of every living thing.
17   The LORD is righteous in all his ways
           and kind in all his works.
18   The LORD is near to all who call on him,
           to all who call on him in truth.
19   He fulfills the desire of those who fear him;
           he also hears their cry and saves them.
20   The LORD preserves all who love him,
           but all the wicked he will destroy.

21   My mouth will speak the praise of the LORD,
           and let all flesh bless his holy name forever and ever.

Reflection

DECEMBER 24
~ Psalm 146

Put Not *Your Trust in Princes*

1 Praise the LORD!
  Praise the LORD, O my soul!
2 I will praise the LORD as long as I live;
    I will sing praises to my God while I have my being.

3 Put not your trust in princes,
    in a son of man, in whom there is no salvation.
4 When his breath departs, he returns to the earth;
    on that very day his plans perish.

5 Blessed is he whose help is the God of Jacob,
    whose hope is in the LORD his God,
6 who made heaven and earth,
    the sea, and all that is in them,
who keeps faith forever;
    who executes justice for the oppressed,
7   who gives food to the hungry.

The LORD sets the prisoners free;
    the LORD opens the eyes of the blind.
8 The LORD lifts up those who are bowed down;
    the LORD loves the righteous.
9 The LORD watches over the sojourners;
    he upholds the widow and the fatherless,
    but the way of the wicked he brings to ruin.

10 The LORD will reign forever,
    your God, O Zion, to all generations.
Praise the LORD!

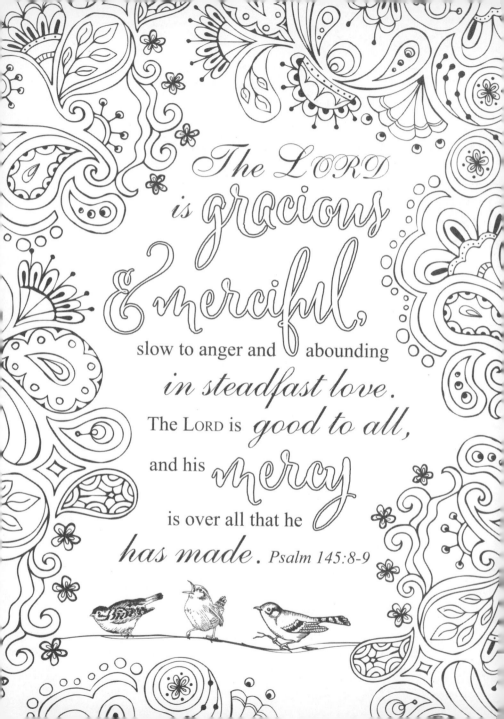

The LORD is gracious & merciful, slow to anger and abounding in steadfast love. The LORD is good to all, and his mercy is over all that he has made. Psalm 145:8-9

DECEMBER 25
~ Psalm 147:1-6

He Heals the Brokenhearted

1 Praise the LORD!
  For it is good to sing praises to our God;
     for it is pleasant, and a song of praise is fitting.
2 The LORD builds up Jerusalem;
     he gathers the outcasts of Israel.
3 He heals the brokenhearted
     and binds up their wounds.
4 He determines the number of the stars;
     he gives to all of them their names.
5 Great is our Lord, and abundant in power;
     his understanding is beyond measure.
6 The LORD lifts up the humble;
     he casts the wicked to the ground.

Reflection

DECEMBER 26
~ Psalm 147:7-13

7   Sing to the LORD with thanksgiving;
        make melody to our God on the lyre!

8   He covers the heavens with clouds;
        he prepares rain for the earth;
        he makes grass grow on the hills.

9   He gives to the beasts their food,
        and to the young ravens that cry.

10   His delight is not in the strength of the horse,
        nor his pleasure in the legs of a man,

11   but the LORD takes pleasure in those who fear him,
        in those who hope in his steadfast love.

12   Praise the LORD, O Jerusalem!
        Praise your God, O Zion!

13   For he strengthens the bars of your gates;
        he blesses your children within you.

Reflection

DECEMBER 27
~ Psalm 147:14-20

14   He makes peace in your borders;
        he fills you with the finest of the wheat.
15   He sends out his command to the earth;
        his word runs swiftly.
16   He gives snow like wool;
        he scatters frost like ashes.
17   He hurls down his crystals of ice like crumbs;
        who can stand before his cold?
18   He sends out his word, and melts them;
        he makes his wind blow and the waters flow.
19   He declares his word to Jacob,
        his statutes and rules to Israel.
20   He has not dealt thus with any other nation;
        they do not know his rules.
        Praise the LORD!

Reflection

DECEMBER 28

Praise the Name of the Lord

1 Praise the LORD!
Praise the LORD from the heavens;
    praise him in the heights!
2 Praise him, all his angels;
    praise him, all his hosts!

3 Praise him, sun and moon,
    praise him, all you shining stars!
4 Praise him, you highest heavens,
    and you waters above the heavens!

5 Let them praise the name of the LORD!
    For he commanded and they were created.
6 And he established them forever and ever;
    he gave a decree, and it shall not pass away.

7 Praise the LORD from the earth,
    you great sea creatures and all deeps,
8 fire and hail, snow and mist,
    stormy wind fulfilling his word!

Reflection

DECEMBER 29
~ Psalm 148:9-14

9   Mountains and all hills,
        fruit trees and all cedars!
10   Beasts and all livestock,
        creeping things and flying birds!

11   Kings of the earth and all peoples,
        princes and all rulers of the earth!
12   Young men and maidens together,
        old men and children!

13   Let them praise the name of the LORD,
        for his name alone is exalted;
        his majesty is above earth and heaven.
14   He has raised up a horn for his people,
        praise for all his saints,
        for the people of Israel who are near to him.
    Praise the LORD!

Reflection

DECEMBER 30
~ Psalm 149

Sing to the Lord a New Song

1 Praise the LORD!
  Sing to the LORD a new song,
    his praise in the assembly of the godly!
2 Let Israel be glad in his Maker;
    let the children of Zion rejoice in their King!
3 Let them praise his name with dancing,
    making melody to him with tambourine and lyre!
4 For the LORD takes pleasure in his people;
    he adorns the humble with salvation.
5 Let the godly exult in glory;
    let them sing for joy on their beds.
6 Let the high praises of God be in their throats
    and two-edged swords in their hands,
7 to execute vengeance on the nations
    and punishments on the peoples,
8 to bind their kings with chains
    and their nobles with fetters of iron,
9 to execute on them the judgment written!
    This is honor for all his godly ones.
  Praise the LORD!

Reflection

DECEMBER 31
~ Psalm 150

Let Everything *Praise the Lord*

1   Praise the Lord!
Praise God in his sanctuary;
    praise him in his mighty heavens!
2   Praise him for his mighty deeds;
    praise him according to his excellent greatness!

3   Praise him with trumpet sound;
    praise him with lute and harp!
4   Praise him with tambourine and dance;
    praise him with strings and pipe!
5   Praise him with sounding cymbals;
    praise him with loud clashing cymbals!
6   Let everything that has breath praise the Lord!
Praise the Lord!

Reflection

Praise the *LORD!*
Praise God in his sanctuary;
praise him in his *mighty*
heavens!
Praise him
for his mighty deeds;
praise him according to his
excellent greatness!

Psalm 150:1-2